The Crystal Skull

The story of the mystery, myth and magic of the Mitchell-Hedges crystal skull discovered in a lost Mayan city during a search for Atlantis

Richard M. Garvin

Doubleday & Company, Inc., Garden City, New York. 1973

ISBN: 0-385-09456-6
Library of Congress Catalog Card Number 72–84912

For Frank and Mabel, of course

Contents

THE CRYSTAL SKULL

THE THING IN THE VAULT

Off and on for the past six years, a vault in a small branch of the Bank of America in a sleepy suburb of San Francisco named Mill Valley, held a clear crystal unlike anything known on earth.

For this is a solid crystal, ground with meticulous care to the size and shape of a human skull. And this enormous gem—for that is exactly what it is—must rank in any record book or almanac of oddities as contender for the title of the world's strangest object.

The everyday world has neither found time nor a way to appreciate this transparent crystal cranium hewn out of a single piece of clear quartz. For though it can be and has been examined in detail, it arouses more bewilderment than scientific curiosity. It is somewhat like the Great

Pyramid: we marvel at its mere existence and, not being able to catalog it accurately in our values, print its picture on a penny postcard.

But the skull is a scientific reality and an exquisite *objet d'art*. At the same time it is shrouded in mysticism and its origins hint at some lost civilizations.

Since its discovery in 1927, the skull has received only a modest amount of publicity—most of it from South Africa where it had been christened the "Skull of Doom."

I first came across the crystal skull several years ago when I was involved in researching another project. A friend of mine, an art director for an advertising agency, mentioned that somewhere in the San Francisco Bay Area there was a crystal ball carved in the form of a human face. I was only mildly interested at the time, but later the idea of such an object scratched at my curiosity. Several months later I decided to track it down. The search led to some rather unorthodox suggestions.

On a tree-lined ridge, where the eye may pan a spectacular sweep of the San Francisco Bay, a man by the name of Frank Dorland occupies a spacious, comfortable and elegant rebuilt farmhouse with his wife, Mabel, and pet cats. This castle is also his studio and laboratory. For Dorland is an art conservator, or restorer, of national prominence. He is also an unhurried humanist, a calm, quiet individual, in command of an excellent sense of humor, a keen mind, and talents reaching beyond his skill as a craftsman for the finest museums and art galleries of the world. His home is brimming with bottles and jars—everywhere there are tubes of rare pigments, cans of resins, bottles of varnish and solvents. Around the studio and adjoining rooms are dozens of priceless paintings in various stages of restoration.

Dorland and I talked for several hours on a foggy Saturday afternoon. He showed me photographs of the skull and told me of his uncanny experiences since the time he first held it some six years ago. His enthusiasm was effusive, and the story of the skull tumbled out of him in a litany of verbal beads, clouded at times with unsupportable speculations, but, nevertheless, somehow believable.

With the characteristic preciseness of his craft, Frank Dorland has examined the crystal skull in utmost detail for these past years. And perhaps as a result of these concentrated labors, he has experienced some reactions from the skull which can only be classified as bordering upon the *outré*.

But I felt as a skeptic. Knowing for certain the answer to a mystery is one thing; communicating it effectively to someone else is quite another matter. To those who are hypersensitive, this is often a rather traumatic thing. These people go away completely wrapped up in their own thoughts, ambiguities and suggestions. They are as crushed men. All vision is lost. But, of course, it is the world which is the loser.

In our computer-synchronized society, hard, cold facts and numbers must be produced for analysis. Otherwise, one is suspect and perhaps branded a liar. But it is almost impossible to convince others of a *mystery* because reason and not lavish display must work in presenting evidence that is indisputable. And there is little hope in appealing to any scientific court of appraisal because most want to leave no stone unturned, when, in truth, they leave many. Thus history is a conglomerate of ill-timed judgments and pitifully sad mistakes. I could simply not believe the incredible things he had told me about the crystal skull. It was a year later when I called on Dorland again.

Twelve months did little to mollify my curiosity. Then, on an icy-cold spring evening, with the wispy fingers of San Francisco fog curling over the high, dark Pacific ridge, I saw the crystal skull for the first time. And I saw it illuminated by candlelight.

How should I describe my reaction? It was like a cold visceral shock—a minute glimpse into the farthest reaches of elsewhere. I felt an ancient contact—a subliminal awareness of something which harked back to the primeval darknesses created by a Poe, a Bierce or a Lovecraft. The crystal skull exuded mystery and excitement. There was no doubt as to its beauty and spectacular craftsmanship. It glistened like an enormous sculptured diamond. And I stood transfixed as the flame of a candle danced a fantastic orange ballet in the sockets of the hollow eyes.

In conversation over coffee later, I learned from Frank Dorland that he had devoted practically every waking hour for the past five years to an intensive study of the skull. He was months behind in his restoration work, but during this time he had photographed the crystal skull with specially constructed cameras and high-powered microscopes. Models of the skull had been cast in both plaster and epoxies, and cross-sections had been cut and measured with precision. During this time, Dorland had also reached some eerie conclusions. "It is not unusual," he told me one time, "for the skull to produce *unexplained* phenomena."

In presenting the problem of the skull to conventional scientists, Dorland has run into innumerable roadblocks. It has been examined by leading academies, and letters attesting to the enigma are on file. But official eyes conveniently turn the other way when it comes to taking a solid position of the skull's history or its importance to archaeology. Many universities have chosen to ignore it simply because they cannot come to grips with the fact that there may be a knowledge demonstrated here which is beyond our civilized comprehension.

Dorland has also been accused of having the skull manufactured for publicity purposes. But that is absurd. The skull is not a fake and of this we are now positive. The ownership of the skull remains with its alleged finder, Anna Le Guillon Mitchell-Hedges. Anna, the adopted daughter of the famed explorer F. A. Mitchell-Hedges, states that she unearthed it in the ancient city of Lubaantún, deep within the jungles of British Honduras.

Why does stipulated science boycott the skull? Why, instead of being in a laboratory under controlled analysis, had it been allowed to reside in the tomblike darkness of a bank vault in the village of Mill Valley, California?

"They have nothing to gain and everything to lose," Dorland speculates. "They have not planned for it in their universities and the last thing they want is some damned object coming into their *sanctum sanctorums* to upset the boat."

The academicians take the exact attitude which confronted Immanuel Velikovsky over two decades ago when he speculated on our earth and our solar system. He was pinned to the wall as a wild man by a science whose theories were in direct opposition to his radical writings. Yet, Velikovsky was vindicated two decades later with the advent of planetary and deep space probes. Science is continually being presented with knowledge our present technology simply cannot explain.

Dorland has also reached the conclusion that this carefully-carved hunk of clear quartz is the granddaddy of all crystal balls—perhaps the only hard evidence of an oracle now in existence.

Ancient man believed that rock crystal of this sort was something like frozen holy water from heaven. Heaven was postulated to be composed of a vast sea of glass, possibly because such a substance defied his belief. Diamonds, rock salt, crystal and glass all went into the same bin: it was all petrified water of some sort, in which imperfections and minute flaws in the crystal symbolized the souls of the departed. It is also known that rock crystal was believed to generate magical powers of the most important kind. As early as 4000 B.C., the Egyptians placed a small circular piece of crystal in the center of the forehead of the deceased prior to mummification. With this artificial third eye, the newly departed could walk into the endless splendors of eternity.

It was because of the mystical nature of quartz crystal that so much time, effort and elbow grease were devoted to its manufacture. Dorland estimates it took at least three hundred years of constant man-labor to grind out the Mitchell-Hedges skull from beginning to end. But, in another and more important sense, there is no end.

The Mitchell-Hedges skull is still changing.

In the relatively few years in which modern science has observed it, the skull has reacted quite differently in different environments. According to Dorland, the Mitchell-Hedges skull was intended to be a unique symbol of wisdom in the universe—the brain box of the cosmos.

Perhaps there is a more realistic reason, which we all hesitate to acknowledge. There are spiritualistic overtones clouding the research of the skull. "Now, I have done my utmost since this thing came into my care," Dorland told me emphatically, "to keep this skull far away from anything on parapsychology, psychic phenomena, spiritualism, and so forth. But that has been a total flop. I have simply been unable to do it. It is a strange, *strange* object. It fascinates people with its hypnotic effect. People of all sorts are drawn to it as if it were a magnet. I have had people look at it and show a tendency to go sound asleep. In others it causes the pulse to quicken. People can see all sorts of things in the skull. It is a crystal ball—perhaps the granddaddy of all crystal balls."

Evidence Dorland has uncovered has caused him to speculate that in all probability, the skull was first carved and put to religious use either by the legendary people of Atlantis or the ancient Egyptians or Babylonians. At that time it resembled the crude specimen on display in the British Museum and was, in a sense, unfinished. Later, it was used by the Babylonian priests in religious temples on the hill of skulls perhaps around 1000 B.C. The Phoenicians then brought the skull from Babylon to Central America where it was used first by the Mayas and then by the Aztecs. Perhaps the skull spent some time at Atlantis before being transported to Central America. It was probably the Maya or Aztecs which completed the sculpting, detached the lower jaw, and carved the prisms into the piece. The skull was then "lost" again for hundreds of years until found by the Mitchell-Hedges expedition.

"During this lost period," Dorland states, "it is quite possible that the skull might have resided in the London temple of the Knights Templar prior to their battle with the Catholics just before the Holy Wars. Descriptions which I have read of the inner sanctum of the Knights Templar mention a head which is sometimes referred to as 'a crystal head with eyes that glow like jewels.' This opens up many possibilities which we can take up later."

Dorland does not close the door on the possibility of

supernatural properties of the skull, however. "There have been strange happenings since it has been in my care. I would like to find out why it does these things. The most astounding thing that has happened is that I saw this glow—an aura, if you wish—around it one evening. Now, I could easily explain that if I had some cocktails before dinner, but there was no liquor in the house. During five of the six years' experiments with the skull, we exercised a discipline that we felt necessary. We used no stimulants or sedatives, to ensure any human reactions would not be traced to the effects of any medical reason. We neither drink nor smoke so that helped as regards the well-known effect of nicotine or alcohol. Our coffee was decaffeinated, our teas were Nettle, Rosehips, Rooebusch and other herb teas. We enjoyed these so much that after the skull left our care, we never stopped the habit of nonuse of any stimulants or sedatives except on rare occasions. The skull was illuminated by ordinary light, but suddenly it grew—this aura—and it continued to grow to about eighteen inches surrounding the skull. It remained there for six minutes or so. Now, if I had a tendency to believe in spiritualism, I might be satisfied that this was a sort of spiritual phenomenon. But I question it. Or now I think I do. I wonder if it reacts in some way to radar?"

Dorland's studio is not far from an air-defense radar installation on nearby Mount Tamalpais. He has postulated that perhaps some sort of radar activity could activate the quartz, perhaps causing some parascientific piezoelectric effect. However, this can probably be safely ruled out since the radar is constantly scanning the atmosphere in a preprogrammed pattern. Further, no such effect is known.

"The aura started out close to the skull with no color in it at all," Dorland explained. "Now the skull has a peculiar lack of color, no trace of a tint. But the aura grew strong with a faint trace of the color of hay, similar to a ring around the moon. It came as such a surprise when I first saw it, that I picked up a magazine to focus my eyes on print to be certain I was not hallucinating. I moved about the room. But the thing stayed there for a good six minutes. It was, naturally, a rather astounding experience to say the least. And it made me want to keep very quiet, as to not disturb it. But what it was, I just simply do not know."

The Mitchell-Hedges skull does not limit itself to visual phenomena alone. "There is another odd property connected with this object," Dorland said. "There have been times, when the skull is out of the vault, that sounds occur around the house. It is much like an *a cappella* choir. No instrumental music, but human voices singing some strange chants in a very soft manner. Then there are the bells. The sounds of bells, sharp and metallic, and quite high. No deep gongs or church bells, these are faint, high-pitched silver bells, very quiet but very noticeable. I have simply no explanation for these things."

Other times, when the skull was kept in his home overnight, mysterious sounds have occurred, various items have been found strewn about when the doors and windows are locked (his home is ultrasecure due to the valuable paintings inside) and there have been other inexplicable phenomena.

Strangely, it *is* possible to see things in the skull due to its veils, impurities and other imperfections. "You can see the damnedest things you ever saw in your life: other skulls, high mountains, fingers and faces. On three occasions, I saw a dark spot appear which grew to cover about one-half of the skull and appeared to be a clear black void surrounded by bands of deep purple. Images of temples appear and disappear. I have photographed these."

In these and other conversations I have had with Frank Dorland over a period of two years, ideas have emerged which hint at lost Atlantis and mysteries which may predate history. And so, within these pages, are presented the findings, speculations and conclusions which he has reached since the crystal skull was first entrusted to his hands.

MASKS OF DOOM?

THE SKULL, it is claimed, was discovered rather recently—in the Lubaantún Tomb, part of the abandoned ruins of an enormous Mayan citadel, in British Honduras. The year was 1927. Now Lubaantún is liana-covered and heavy with vegetation. The city that sacrificed to build such monuments to future generations—without the aid of the wheel, supposedly—was long ago forsaken for some forgotten reason.

The skull was found underneath a collapsed altar by Anna Mitchell-Hedges. Her adopted father, F. A. Mitchell-Hedges, was a noted explorer and had spent the past five years searching South America for Lubaantún and for evidence of a lost Atlantis near the Bay Islands off the coastline of Honduras.

It is his story that Anna discovered the skull on her seventeenth birthday. This could be the truth, a romantic coincidence, or an important clue to its real origin. Mitchell-Hedges, in the first edition of his autobiography, *Danger My Ally*, wrote that "how the skull came into my possession I have reason for not revealing." Curiously, this statement was deleted from later editions.

Studies of the skull were started by Frank Dorland in 1956 although it was not until October 19, 1964, that the skull was entrusted to Dorland and brought to him in New York City. Since that time, Dorland—an expert on religious icons—has been trying to determine what it is and what it is not.

Then, in November of 1970, the skull was abruptly taken from him by Anna. In a hasty dispatch, she boarded a Greyhound bus and returned with the skull to her home in Ontario.

The skull is a skillfully crafted piece of realistic sculpture, beautifully clouded with veils and bubbles encapsulated when that mineral was formed eons ago. Apparently it was carved without the aid of metal-age tools since no telltale concentric scratches have been identified through high-power microscopes and other tests Dorland has conducted.

But the piece itself offers a beautiful balance and an almost natural purity. It exhibits a harmony of line, mass and surface. Strangely, the zygomatic arches (the arch of the bone that extends along the front or side of the skull) are relieved and separated from the skull itself. These arches, using principles amazingly similar to our modern optic technology, act as "light pipes" to channel light from the base of the skull into the excavated eye sockets. Here they terminate in miniature concave lenses that focus the beam to the rear of the sockets themselves.

Evidence of an even more mysterious nature is found in both the hand-ground and natural prisms and lenses, which also channel illumination from the base and distribute images and light. A set of concave and convex lenses gather light rays focused at the base of the skull and transmit them directly into the eye sockets.

Thus, if the skull was suspended, say over a hollow altar, and a flame lit beneath it, most of the illumination would be reflected in the eyes of the skull, causing them to flicker eerily. When Dorland duplicates this experiment, the skull "lights up like it was on fire."

Dorland has discovered that other "tricks" have been built into the skull. The jawbone fits snugly into two polished sockets and can be wiggled up and down. The skull itself balances at a point where two tiny bearing holes are drilled on each side of its base and bottom. It seems to have been skillfully designed to receive counterweights. If the skull were placed on a hollow altar with all its mechanisms working, this would be the picture: its eyes would flicker and glow wildly; the jaw would open and close; the head would nod approval or disapproval with the barest breath of air—a macabre, animated sibyl.

Finally, an interior ribbon prism can be seen when look-

ing into the upper surface. The prism can be used to
magnify and view objects held beneath the skull. And
tiny focused pinpoints of light, also discovered by Dorland,
are projected from the rear of the eye sockets.

Dorland wonders if contrivances of this kind might not
be the mark of a civilization on the skids—for all its
technical virtuosity. Why else should such painstaking care
be devoted to the construction of a magician's prop unless
it was the type of prop which could keep the masses
under control by trickery and semireligious magnetism?

Dorland also feels that the skull may have had great
influence on history, because the statutes and regulations
of whatever strange society constructed it were likely
to have been made by priests, not by elected governments
and the military. Conceivably, the government itself was
closely controlled by the crystal oracle and its manip-
ulators.

Mineralogical and morphological examinations conducted by Dorland and others have determined that the
piece was carved from a single block of clear quartz.
Roughly, it measures 5 inches high by 7 inches long and
it is 5 inches wide. It weighs 11 pounds, 7 ounces, and it is
valued in excess of a quarter-million dollars. But it is, of
course, priceless.

At first, the mysterious crystal skull was thought to be
a mate to another crystal discovered in Mexico in 1889
and now preserved in the Department of Ethnography

of the British Museum in London. That skull has been classified as pre-Columbian—probably Aztec or Mixtec.* However, it was soon noted that the Mitchell-Hedges skull was more detailed and refined in design than the earlier find. Indeed, there was quite a difference: this one had moving parts and its surface gleamed with a strange interior luster. But they were also quite similar, and it is their similarity which raises some intriguing questions.

Little has been written about the British Museum specimen and even less has appeared in anthropological journals. For the most part it has been ignored by the British Museum and regarded solely as a curiosity hauled out of Mexico by an officer of Maximilian's army before the French occupation.

Its first and perhaps most comprehensive description comes from the text of G. F. Kunz who published the following in *Gems and Precious Stones* in New York in 1890:

> Rock crystal has not, in our time at least, been discovered, in Mexico or Central America, of a quality or of sufficient quantity to be of much use to the arts, yet there have been found a number of interesting prehistoric objects made of rock crystal—skulls from 1 inch

---

* There is also a smaller skull, about half the size of the Mitchell-Hedges specimen, at the Musée de l'homme, Palais de Chaillot, in Paris. It is believed to have been the ornament at the end of a staff and probably represents Mictlantecutli, the Aztec god of death. It, too, has been classified as Aztec, and it measures approximately 4⁵⁄₁₆ inches in height; the lowest part measures 5⅞ inches and it weighs 5 pounds, 8½ ounces.

to 7 inches in width, crescents, beads, and other articles
—of which the material is excellent, and the workman-
ship equal to anything done by the early lapidaries.
Small skulls are in the Blake Collection at the United
States National Museum, the Douglas Collection, New
York, the British Museum, and the Trocadero Museum.

A large skull, now in the possession of George H.
Sission of New York, is very remarkable. . . . The eyes
are deep hollows; the line separating the upper from
the lower row of teeth has evidently been produced
by a wheel made to revolve by a spring held in the hand,
or possibly by a string stretched across a bow, and is
very characteristic of Mexican work. Little is known of
its history and nothing of its origin. It was brought
from Mexico by a Spanish officer sometime before the
French occupation of Mexico, and was sold to an Eng-
lish collector, at whose death it passed into the hands of
E. Boban, of Paris, and then became the property of Mr.
Sission.

That such large worked objects of rock crystal are
not found in Mexico might lead one to infer its possible
Chinese or Japanese origin. But it is evident that the
workmanship of the skull is not Chinese or Japanese, or
nature would have been more closely copied; and if the
work were of European origin, it would undoubtedly
have been more carefully finished in some minor details.
Prof. Edward S. Morse of Salem, Mass., who resided
in Japan for several years, and Tatui Baba of Japan,
now of New York City, state positively that this skull
is not of Japanese origin. Mr. Baba gives as one reason
for his belief that the Japanese would never cut such an
object as a skull from so precious a material.

In ancient Mexico there was undoubtedly a veneration for skulls, for we find not only small skulls of rock crystal, notably the one in the Cristy Collection in the British Museum, incrusted with turquoise, and it may have been one of these that suggested the making of this skull, the one at the Trocadero Museum, and the smaller one. Two very interesting crescents are known, the one in the Trocadero Museum, the other in the collection of Dr. Maxwell Sommerville, in the Metropolitan Museum of Art, New York City. Beads of this material are sometimes found in the tombs with jadeite and other stone beads. They rarely have a diameter of an inch.

Rock crystal in large masses has been reported from near Pachuca, Hidalgo, in the state of Michoacan, and in veins near La Paza in Lower (Baja) California; the center of the vein is said to be beautifully pellucid, but the sides are opaque white. It is not known whether the rock crystal used by the aboriginees was obtained at a Mexican locality, or whether it came from Calavaras County, Calif., where masses of rock crystal are found containing vermicular procholorite inclusions identical with those observed in the large skull described above.

TWO SKULLS

In July 1936, the British Museum and Mitchell-Hedges skulls were compared by G. M. Morant in *Man*, a monthly record of anthropological science published under the direction of the Royal Anthropological Institute of Great Britain and Ireland.

Morant compared the two skulls from a purely morphological point of view. He noted many similar features including an almost perfect bilateral symmetry, the absence of any suture marks or seams on the top of the cranium. In addition, there is a significant absence of glabellar prominence or superciliary ridges suggesting that—in both cases—the skull is that of a female. In addition, Morant noted a slight curvature of the median sagittal sections or the bilateral symmetrical plane repre-

COMPARISON OF PHYSICAL MEASUREMENTS
(Owing to the absence of sutures, only a few of the usual
measurements can be taken accurately)

Measurement	British Museum specimen	Mitchell-Hedges specimen
Glabellar-occipital length:	117 mm.	174 mm.
Maximum calvarial breadth:	135 mm.	140 mm.
Cephalic index:	76.3 mm.	80.5 mm.
Bizygomatic breadth:	117 mm.	117 mm.
Nasal breadth:	22 mm.	24 mm.
Breadth of left orbit:	34.5 mm.	37.5 mm.
Height of left orbit:	37 mm.	33.5 mm.
Left orbital index:	107.2 mm.	89.3 mm.

sented by an imaginary line from the tip of the nose, tip
of the chin and the back of the head, and the absence
of any indication of the position of the lambda or the
angle of junction of lambdoid and sagittal sutures.

In the Mitchell-Hedges skull, the median section of
the front region is slightly more protruding than that of
the British specimen, but it appears highly unlikely that
the skull from which it was copied was deformed. The
brain boxes of both skulls seem to be quite well filled.

There are several unusual features common to both
specimens: the unnatural straightness of the media sections
of the facial skeletons, the prominence of the anterior

nasal spines and the verticality of the rami of the mandibles seen from in front.

Marked differences between the two specimens are noted in the conformation of the facial and basal regions. The Mitchell-Hedges skull has a separate, articulated jawbone and "in a word, the facial part of the British Museum specimen is a crude representation" of the Mitchell-Hedges skull.

In the British specimen, the orbits are unnaturally round and no great attempt had been made to excavate the zygomatic arches or the bone which extends along the front or side of the skull beneath the orbit. In the Mitchell-Hedges skull these are quite well defined. Further, the Mitchell-Hedges skull shows the definite shape of separate teeth while no attempt was made to realistically sculpture this in the British skull. All over, the Mitchell-Hedges skull is a far cry from the crude, rough configurations of the British specimen. In fact, it could be considered a blank or the first rough sketch by its creator.

It is interesting to superimpose the outlines of both skulls. Trackings made from photographs show that the brain boxes diverge to an appreciable extent, but certainly no more than any two random skulls picked for examination. The orbits are not far apart and Morant concludes that the outlines of the lower jaws, the teeth lines and the nasal apertures are practically coincident. The breadth at the zygomatic arches are identical, but the forms of the arches are slightly different. Further, the close correspondence between the two outlines is again remarkable.

According to Morant, this comparison makes it impossible to "avoid the conclusion that the crystal skulls are not of independent origin. It is almost inconceivable that two artificers, having no connection with one another, and using different human skulls as models, should have produced specimens so closely similar in form as these two are."[1]

Morant's opinion is that they are representations of the same skull, but he agrees that one may have been copied from the other. Essentially, the only difference between them is due to the fact that the British skull is crude when compared to the well-defined and highly detailed Mitchell-Hedges specimen.

On the other hand, some technologists may argue that if one were the copy of the other, then the more finished would be the later specimen. But Morant does not accept this. "If we suppose that the British specimen was modeled from a human skull, and that at some later date the original crystal was copied by another craftsman who used another human skull to guide him in making some features more realistic. But this craftsman must have had some knowledge of anatomy, for otherwise the substitution of a false model for the real one would have been very likely to lead to some anatomical abnormalities in his product, although none are actually observed [sic]."[2]

Morant concludes his argument with the suggestion that the skull is more orthognathous (not having the lower parts of the jaw project) than the average European cranium. For example, an American Indian skull would probably possess a more projecting jawbone and a broader and higher facial skeleton. But interracial variation is so great that such conclusions are highly speculative.

Adrian Digby of the British Museum considered at some length the implications of Morant's opinion that the two skulls are related and perhaps were of the same origin. Digby pointed out three possibilities: (1) Morant is correct in assuming that they were made at the same time; (2) the Mitchell-Hedges skull was made from the original and the British Museum skull was made at a later time from a civilization not acquainted with anatomical details; (3) the British skull was the original and the Mitchell-Hedges skull the copy.

Digby points out that each postulation contains its inherent difficulties. If both skulls originated from the same models, then why is there so much difference between the two? It would be difficult to assume that the same civilization spawned two skulls with such sculptural differences.

Digby also notes that in terms of the stylistic differences they are not contemporary. "This means that the original 'source' skull was a particularly important skull, probably belonging to a culture hero or warrior, a 'museum piece,' as it were, to which various craftsmen would have access, or alternatively that the skull was the property of a particular family of craftsmen, and that one model was made by a descendant of the maker of the others. Dr. Morant draws particular attention to the feminine or infantile characteristics of both skulls, so it is unlikely that the model is based on a 'museum piece,' for such a skull would almost certainly be a representation of the deathgod, a male character, or of a warrior. But the writer [Digby] can conceive no other set of circumstances which would without the use of pure coincidence, account for different craftsmen at different times having access to the same original."[3]

In its examination—nearly forty years ago—it was found that "in neither case is there any trace of identifiable tool marks, and it is certain that neither specimen was made with steel tools."[4]

Digby comments further on the suggestion that the British specimen was copied from the Mitchell-Hedges skull. Certainly it is not unusual in copying for the piece to contain errors and a substantial amount of degeneration. It is certainly possible that the British specimen is the great grandchild of the Mitchell-Hedges skull.

There are difficulties here also. The British skull is "traditionally correct" insofar as it is most like other skulls, particularly Mexican and South American. In view of this, it is Digby's comment that the Mitchell-Hedges skull was "improved on." "But it is extraordinary that anybody wishing to carve a skull out of rock crystal, and taking a real skull as his model, should modify its dimensions to fit those of another crystal skull which he would see was but a poor copy of nature. It shows a perverted ingenuity such as one would expect to find in a forger, but the Mitchell-Hedges skull bears no traces of recent [metal age] workmanship; so this suggestion may almost certainly be dismissed."[5]

Although Morant's profile comparison of the two skulls is impressive, there is the inherent difficulty in orienting the two crystals in the same plane. Digby points out that there are no key points to help orient the skull either on the Frankfort or Thompson plane. Morant superimposed the profiles and oriented them until they all seemed to follow the same pattern. This made the frontal portion of the Mitchell-Hedges skull higher than that of the British specimen and the basal regions low. But "if, instead, two profiles are superimposed so that the two outlines of the brain box portion of the skull coincide as nearly as possible it will be found that the lower portions of the zygomatic arches are more nearly parallel, and the face becomes more orthognathous, and therefore slightly more European in type than the Museum specimen."[6]

But Digby concedes that it would be extremely rash to suggest that the skulls were of European rather than Mexican manufacture.

The article in *Man* concludes with the comments of H. J. Braunholts, also of the British Museum: "The cranium [of the British Museum specimen] has a perfectly smooth contour, the eyes are circular, and the teeth merely indicated. These peculiarities are in accordance with the general character of ancient Mexican art. It would be hard to quote a single specimen [in] which anatomical detail is fully and faithfully recorded without some degree of 'stylization.' This is particularly the case with the Aztec stone masks and figures of deities, most of which are highly conventional."[7]

The Mitchell-Hedges skull pays "considerable attention to the correct rendering of detail; minor protruberances on the cranium are carefully modeled . . . such realism seems beyond the ordinary range of Aztec art, and gives the skull the character almost of an anatomical study in a scientific age."[8]

Since that time, the Mexican government (who suggest it is Mixtec in origin) have tried unsuccessfully to have the skull returned to them. The British skull aroused more than its share of curiosity, and in 1967 it was removed from display by Dr. A. E. Werner, head of the museum's laboratory. Rumor spread that it was because it was discovered to be a fake. A report was promised, but to date no further information has been released by the museum.

Looking back now, over almost four decades, Digby has changed his views, and he now believes that both skulls were made for the same purpose at about the same time. He thinks it's most likely that they are pre-Columbian and might belong to some masonic cult. He does not think there is any likelihood that they were ever of Japanese origin as some have suggested.[9]

In its physical construction, Dorland claims to have found evidences of two distinct stages of evolution. First, there was the rough cut—the stage in which the skull at the British Museum is forever fixed. The second stage was the detailing of the skull's features and the intricate carving of a series of lenses and prisms into the base of the skull, across the center of the brain cavity, and at the rear of the eye sockets. Even though experts at the British Museum and other institutions had been inspecting the Mitchell-Hedges skull for years, these surprising details were never noticed until Dorland came into possession of it.

It is important to remember that the skull has been tentatively identified as Mayan only because it was found in Mayan territory. Dorland estimates, however, that the skull could be centuries older than that; and on this assumption, it must belong to a civilization that existed long before that enigmatic race inhabited the Caribbean area. But there is no real way to prove or disprove any of the "when" theories.

Rock crystal cannot be subjected to carbon-14 dating tests since this method is only valuable on such organic materials such as bone or wood fossils. And while it is true that tiny encapsulated bits of water (which could be tested by other methods) are contained within the crystal, examination would necessitate the destruction of the piece —an obvious impossibility. Further, crystal does not change with age like other materials. Carbon-14 dating is quite inaccurate when it comes to dating prehistorical objects. It can be in error as much as 50 per cent for objects five thousand years and older. In addition, quartz crystal does not corrode, become brittle, attract organisms or acquire a patina. Centuries pass without affecting it. It has been postulated that using some dating and analytical techniques the location of the original quartz quarry could possibly be determined. But the search would be impractical and economically prohibitive. But even if we could date this material it would be of little help: we would be dating the crystal and not the crystal skull.

But skulls have been recurring symbols and objects of veneration from man's primeval days—in varying degrees representing death, destruction, rebirth, knowledge and wisdom of the highest order. Thousands of sculptures and castings of the human cranium have survived to our era. Yet this skull is ground out of a rare material: clear rock crystal of unusual size. While it is not difficult to find rock crystal in larger and heavier pieces, inevitably they are not clear but tinted amber, green or pink. Most Chinese rock crystal, for example, is of a dirty tan color. Clarity of color was always sought after, for we know that in ancient rituals the lucidity of the crystal was of prime importance.

But, as Dorland suggests, the Mitchell-Hedges skull might date back to ancient Babylon, Egypt or even Tibet. Of course, we will never know. In all probability, there are other crystal skulls scattered around the globe. But none has yet been uncovered which can compare in beauty and workmanship to the Mitchell-Hedges find.

◎◎◎◎◎◎◎◎◎◎◎◎◎◎◎◎◎◎◎◎◎◎◎◎◎

four

MITCHELL-HEDGES:
MAN IN SEARCH OF A MYTH

ATLANTIS WAS NO MYTH BUT THE CRADLE
OF CIVILIZATON, DECLARES HEDGES

IN 1935, the *New York American* blasted the noted
explorer's name once again into national prominence. F. A.
Mitchell-Hedges was on the trail of the lost Atlantis
and no public relations man could have done a better job
than Mitchell-Hedges himself.

"Atlantis existed," he wrote. "Its engulfment caused
'The Flood,' a cataclysm that wiped out millions. In-
cluded was this advanced cultural race. Here upon Atlantis
was the 'Cradle of Civilization,' which we follow to this
day, and land of origin of the races of America."[10]

The lure of adventure and lost civilizations were an

obsession to Frederick A. Mitchell-Hedges. He grew into
a tall, gaunt man whose pipe was invariably clenched
between thin, tight lips. He was a ruthless believer in
independence at any cost and one who constantly scratched
at those he loved to refer to as "armchair scientists."
Until the day he died, he believed he had found Atlantis
and had pieced together the history of the dawn of man.

His father, John Hedges, was a respected member of
the financial community—a meticulous man who operated
his life with programmed discipline. But since his earliest
days, Mike, as he was called, yearned to be free of a heavily
structured society.

He attended the University School on Gower Street
in London, but the years, in his opinion, were wasted.
He despaired of the too-rigid curriculum and every hour
was spent in pouring over the novels of H. Rider Hag-
gard, Robert Louis Stevenson and the accounts of lost
lands and prehistoric animals conjured up by Arthur
Conan Doyle. Through his psyche trekked the heros of
fiction and the fabulous searches for hidden cities in the
hot, sweaty vegetation of the Mato Grosso. But in particular, he was lured to the ancient civilizations of the
Aztecs, Toltecs and Mayas. This, he concluded, would
be the focal point of his life.

The first opportunity for adventure came sooner than
he thought. Shortly after he had turned sixteen, a friend
of his father, a man named Brooke Mee, was organizing
an expedition into Norway. Jokingly one afternoon, Mee
suggested that Mike might want to come along. Much

to his father's dismay, Mike took the invitation in dead seriousness. Although his father forbade him he finally caved in and gave his approval, hoping the adventure would erase the wanderlust from his system once and for all.

The next three weeks were a flurry of activity: clothing had to be purchased, fishing gear, guns and supplies had to be loaded on board. When all was ready, the expedition set out for Trondheim, a moderate-sized seaport a third of the way up the western coast of Norway.

Tirelessly, he explored the back streets and waterfronts, down curving alleys past sidewalk cafes. Finally, exhausted, he reluctantly returned to the hotel only to notice that his bed was occupied.

"There, to my horror," he wrote later, "fast asleep, her arms above her head, her yellow hair sprawled across the pillow like a scarf, was a girl."[11]

He went downstairs and complained to the room clerk. With typical Nordic casualness the eyes betrayed no surprise. He shrugged his shoulders. "If you vant her . . . have her. If you don't vant . . . she is charged on the bill just the same."

Dumfounded, Mike returned to the room and, against the girl's protestations, asked her to leave. The local custom of providing a companion for the guest provided much laughter at the breakfast table the next morning.

Then, in the vastness of the Arctic, Mitchell-Hedges got his first taste of high adventure. Nights were spent transfixed by the northern lights feathering the night sky.

And there, in the northland, Mitchell-Hedges acquired his first rough knowledge of sex.

And so he returned to London with high hopes of becoming an explorer. He envisioned himself experienced and ready to head an expedition. But qualified archaeologists, scientists, botanists and anthropologists were not in short supply. In the vernacular of the times they were "ten a penny." And he was but seventeen. So, reluctantly, he took a job at his father's stockbrokers. But every shilling, every sixpence he earned was carefully put aside as escape money. Mike and his father continued to disagree and it turned into a stormy relationship at best. And so, in February 1900, he stood alone on the Liverpool docks; his sole possession was a battered suitcase and a few hundred pounds. He was headed for Canada and fortune.

In Montreal he happened upon a man named Clarence McCuaig who convinced him that in order to really make money he would have to go to New York. *But New York was in the wrong direction.* Gold had been discovered in the Klondike. However, it turned out that McCuaig was an influential man in New York's financial establishment. He gave Mike a letter of introduction which he reluctantly took with him on a New York-bound train to cast his lot with the gamblers of the stone jungle.

Almost before he knew it, the letter introduced him directly to J. P. Morgan, and between playing poker and buying the right properties he was able to save ten thousand dollars. He began to make plans for South

America, but his mother fell ill and he had to return home.

In England, he met and married Lilian—Dolly, as he called her—and busied himself making money. The childless years flew by and looking back over his marriage, he knighted himself as "The World's Worst Husband."

He made and lost fortunes many times. Finally fed up with business, he secured Dolly in a small cottage and without a cent to his name decided to go to the Americas. November of 1913 found Mike, now thirty-one, penniless in the lowland bayous of Louisiana.

For months he bummed around the Southern states trying to scrape up enough money to get across the border and down into Central America. He drove himself hard, playing poker and trying his luck at being a ranch hand. But he soon tired of this life, the lure of the Mayas stronger than ever. He had to do something and so he chose Pat Shane's garish gambling casino as the place to try his final throw.

But as usual he had a plan. Biding his time, he waited near the roulette table until a sucker, obviously drunk and rich, tried his luck. And knowing Pat Shane's for what it was, Mitchell-Hedges simply bet against the sucker. As usual the drunk began to win. But as his bets increased, and the casino's crooked wheel began to be employed, Mitchell-Hedges simply bet the opposite color. When the house won the sucker's hundred-dollar bill, there was little concern to pay Mitchell-Hedges five or ten dollars.

So, by the time the drunk had been relieved of every

cent he had, Mitchell-Hedges was five hundred dollars richer. Needless to say Pat Shane was not so subtle in discouraging the future patronage of Mitchell-Hedges. But feeling eager and free at last, he climbed into his ancient automobile and aimed himself toward Mexico.

He had been in Mexico but a week when, relaxing in a cantina, he became aware of men yelling and shouting. Suddenly a posse swung into the courtyard, led by a man in a well-worn shirt with crisscrossed bandoliers. He came straight to Mitchell-Hedges and pushed his large floppy sombrero back from his brow so that he could see a deep groove left by the bullet that had carried away his eye. Then another man crashed the butt of his revolver on his head and a tunnel of unconsciousness closed around him.

He awoke in shock. Not so much from the blow, but from the sudden realization that he had been taken prisoner by one of the most desperate *hombres* in history: Pancho Villa.

Here he was with the desperado—a man with a price on his head so great that the United States government was considering breaking off diplomatic relations with Mexico and massing troops on the border. Villa hated Americans because a dishonest cattleman had cheated him, and Villa was going to kill Mitchell-Hedges.

Pleading *"Ingleese, Ingleese, Ingleese!"* Mitchell-Hedges finally persuaded Villa that he was an Englishman, not an American. And then, at gunpoint, Mitchell-Hedges threw in with Villa and his men.

He found that being a desperado was not quite so bad
after all. Riding with Villa silently under the stars with a
man who knew every trail and the location of every herd
of cattle along the Rio Grande was exciting. It was
impossible for him to suppress the thrill of working with
an experienced rustler or to forget the dusty smell of
the horses or the scent and squeak of saddle leather in
the Mexican badlands.

But it was soon to end. At last the United States took
decisive action against Villa, and General Pershing mar-
shalled twelve thousand troops on the Mexican frontier.
Further, Britain was now at war with Germany and
Mitchell-Hedges pleaded that England needed his services.
To his surprise, Villa agreed.

And so, several weeks later, late in the year of 1914,
Mitchell-Hedges reached London. But because of a leg
wound suffered in Mexico, he was classified as "totally
exempt." He busied himself with volunteer work.

As the war dragged on, once again Mitchell-Hedges
returned to North America. And it was in Port Colborne,
Ontario—late in the summer of 1917—that he met her.
It was at a hotel where he happened to strike up a conversation with two visiting Americans. As the rye whisky
flowed freely, the Americans grew increasingly morose
about their parting. The object of their sorrow was a
ten-year-old orphan girl named Anna-Marie Le Guillon.

Suddenly they began to insist that Mitchell-Hedges take
care of her. "Poor li'l monkey!" said one. "All alone in the

world, nobody to look after her. Crying shame, that's what it is."

Mitchell-Hedges begged off, protesting, "I'm just the right sort of solid stable character! I'd make a sweet parent, I would."

With that he left, went upstairs and packed his suitcase. But ten minutes later the Americans were at his door with the skinny little girl in black stockings. Then someone thrust a battered suitcase at him, mumbled something about keeping her warm and left immediately. Mitchell-Hedges' first reaction was one of anger and surprise. But when he looked at the forlorn little face, words choked in his throat.

Soon thereafter, Anna-Marie and Mitchell-Hedges were established in his apartment in New York. Anna was small and thin, almost pathetic in her appearance. She had yet to smile or even talk with him. Yet there was something about the waif that made Mitchell-Hedges want to do something. He rejected any thought of abandoning her or putting her in an orphanage. They would have to make it together; there simply was no other choice for him.

And that was the way he met his beloved Anna-Marie, who, a decade later, would discover the crystal skull.

With the end of the war, Mitchell-Hedges found himself with a healthy bank balance and an inflexible determination to ramble again. He decided on Spanish Honduras. Anna-Marie, who he now called "Sammy," had

blossomed under his care and a true bond of friendship
had developed between them.

Much to her disappointment, he decided to put Sammy
in a boarding school; but at the last minute he had a
change of heart and said, "Okay, Sammy, we'll stick
together. Don't worry."

They sent a wire to the school informing them of the
change. Anna flung her arms around his neck, her eyes
wet with happy tears.

Mitchell-Hedges was thirty-seven and Sammy was
twelve when they set out for Mexico and Amapala, then
up the mountains to Tegucigalpa. But traveling with
Sammy proved to be a mistake. The country was too
dangerous and, reluctantly, he sent her back to New York
to stay with a friend as he pressed on.

For the next two years he set about to explore Central
America—driven by his consuming interest in Atlantis,
which he thought to be off the coast of Honduras,
probably near the Bay Islands.

Out of the vast, unexplored jungles, the Indians brought
legends of mysterious burned cities, grotesque customs
and tales of strange tribes unknown to the civilized world.
In addition, he had also developed a passion for deep-sea
fishing and had convinced himself that monsters of enormous size lurked in the deep South American waters.
But he would need special equipment to snare them and
so, in spring of 1921, he returned to England to organize
a full-fledged expedition.

After several failures to raise the funds, luck sided up

to him once again. He chanced to meet a woman, one
Lady Richmond Brown—"Mabs"—whose doctors had sol-
emnly sentenced her to death. With nothing to lose, Lady
Richmond Brown pleaded to go with him. "I'm serious,"
she said. "If I'm going to die, I might as well die doing
something worthwhile as living like a vegetable."

And so Mabs went with him. And, as fate would have
it, she did not die, but proved to be a strong, faithful
and uncomplaining inamorata for Mitchell-Hedges.

In September of that year, they set sail from England,
carrying the most advanced fishing gear ever to leave
England. In Panama they bought a twenty-ton yacht,
the *Cara*, and, loaded with food, guns and more equipment,
set sail again. The expedition had begun. The islands—
Neadupo, Oocoopsenekee, Maragandee, Allegandee, Oosto-
opo, Sangandee and Tigre—were visited and explored.
Deep in the bush houses of San Blas they lived with the filth
and poverty, hunger and rotting sores.

During a visit with the Chucunaque, Mitchell-Hedges
encountered his first incredible find.

He had been warned that sickness was rampant throughout the area but he was totally unprepared for the immense amount of disease and poverty vested among the
Chucunaque. The Indians were virtually rotting on their
feet. Not only was the entire tribe affected with a form
of itch which caused their hair to fall from their heads
and sores to cover their bodies, but many of the Indians
were half deaf because the disease had penetrated their
eardrums.

Trachoma was everywhere. Children were affected with hookworm and chiggers—a parasite which lays its eggs under the toenails and causes blood poisoning. Smallpox was also prevalent. In one hut they found an entire family all dead from it.

Mabs and Mitchell-Hedges did the best they could to help the Indians, but it was a losing battle. They could only stand the appalling stench and the hideous appearance of the Indians for short periods.

Under the bitter protestations of the village witch doctor they disposed of his macabre collection of crocodile's teeth, colored stones, carved wooden fetishes and secret herbs. And the disposal was carried out in such a manner that they were able to bring back to England a collection of Chucunaque Indian fetishes unequaled in the history of exploration. And one fetish was so bizarre that it all but defies belief. It was used by the witch doctor only when the patient was near death. It was also restricted to males and if the patient survived it would be considered a miracle by the rest of the villagers. Upon examination it was found to be a human male fetus.

The incredible thing about it is that it was carefully examined by Professor Sir Arthur Keith, F.R.S., a highly regarded anthropologist at the time, who judged it to have been from five to six months old when it was removed from the mother's womb. In some unknown fashion it had been perfectly preserved in its original condition. Every detail from the pores in the skin to the tiny wisps which would have become eyebrows could be seen.

Contrary to the living conditions and the habits of the Chucunaque, such an ability to preserve this embryonic child displays a scientific knowledge far surpassing their technological ability. Further examination revealed it had not been dried, cured, smoked or preserved by any process known a half-decade ago.

Some years later, Mitchell-Hedges made the eerie disclosure that "subsequent close examination disclosed that the fetus had a skull formation hitherto entirely unknown.

"When we were told by experts that it was probably the only specimen of its kind in the world, we felt its proper place was in the British Museum, to which we gladly presented it."[12]

During their voyages in the Caribbean, Mitchell-Hedges and Mabs became increasingly aware of persistent legends regarding a lost city deep within the jungles of British Honduras. Of course tales of such cities are not unusual in Central and South America and hundreds of sites in the Yucatán alone await the archaeologist's spade.

But somehow these rang with authenticity. That added to the fact that Mitchell-Hedges was now convinced that among the Bay Islands lay the fragments of Atlantis. Possibly, he surmised, there was a link between the two.

And so they returned to England to prepare for a major expedition into the interior of British Honduras in search for such a lost city. And a year later, the *Cara* was on its way again.

THE DISCOVERY OF
LUBAANTÚN—
THE CITY OF FALLEN STONES

BRITISH HONDURAS lies on the Caribbean coast of Central America, bounded on the north and part of the west by Mexico, and by Guatemala on the remainder of the west and south. The inner coastal waters are sheltered by a line of reefs, dotted with islets called *cayos*, extending almost the entire length of the colony. There is a low coastal plain, much of it covered with mangrove swamp, but the land rises gradually toward the interior. To the south, the Maya Mountains and the Cockscombs run parallel with the coast, and farther inland is the Mountain Pine Ridge ranging to thirty-three hundred feet above sea level. The greatest part of the mainland is under dense forest.

Little is known of the early history of the area, but the

numerous ruins indicate that for hundreds of years it was heavily populated by the Maya Indians whose comparatively advanced civilization probably reached its zenith between 300 A.D. and 900 A.D. Thereafter, for reasons not fully understood, the civilization collapsed and many of the people migrated elsewhere.

In 1502 Columbus sailed into and named the Bay of Honduras, though he did not actually visit the area which later became British Honduras. The first recorded European settlement was in 1638, by shipwrecked British sailors, later augmented by disbanded British soldiers and sailors after the capture of Jamaica from Spain in 1655. The settlement, whose main activity was logwood cutting, had a troubled history for the next century and a half, being subjected to frequent attacks from the neighboring Spanish settlement. Spain, with papal sanction, claimed sovereignty over the whole of the New World except for the regions of South America assigned to Portugal.

It was not until 1763, under the Treaty of Paris, that Spain, while retaining sovereignty over Belize, the capital, conceded to the British settlers the right to engage in the logwood industry. This was reaffirmed by the Treaty of Versailles in 1783 and the area of the logwood concession was extended by the Convention of London in 1786. Nevertheless, Spanish attacks continued until a decisive victory was won by the settlers, with British naval support, in the Battle of St. George's Cay in 1798. After this, British *de facto* control over the settlement gradually

increased and in 1862 British Honduras was recognized
by Britain as a British colony.

From an early date, the people of the settlement had
governed themselves under a system of primitive democ-
racy by public meeting. A constitution based on this
system was granted in 1765, and with one short interval
continued until 1840, when an executive council was
created. In 1853, the public meeting was finally superseded
by a legislative assembly and when the settlement became
a colony in 1862 a lieutenant-governor was put in control.

In 1871 the crown colony system of government was
introduced and the legislative assembly, by its own vote,
was replaced by a nominated legislative council with an
official majority, presided over by the lieutenant-governor.
The administrative connection with Jamaica ceased in 1884,
when the title of lieutenant-governor was changed to that
of governor.

In 1924, Mitchell-Hedges, along with Lady Richmond
Brown and Dr. Thomas Gann, a crotchety ex-medical
officer of British Honduras and a student of the Maya,
informed the governor of British Honduras of their intent
to search for and excavate the unknown city they were
now convinced existed. A special meeting of the legislative council was held and an act was passed granting them
sole concession for twenty years. And so, at the capital
city of Belize, they took a dugout south to Punta Gorda.

At Punta Gorda, a tiny Indian settlement one hundred
miles south of Belize, they enlisted every able male in the
village to take them into the interior. For months, axes

flashed in the sunlight and trees tumbled to the ground. But finally they stumbled upon the city—overgrown with foliage and resembling an enormous mound of carefully carved stones. They set fire to the thickly matted brush and vines that covered the city and as the holocaust swept onward, walls, terraces and mounds came into view. The pyramids and courtyards of the main citadel of the fallen city shimmered through the bluish smoke.

The tangle of heavy brush vanished into a horizon no white man had ever seen. In the other direction, walls of impenetrable jungle confronted them with the danger of raw wilderness. Beyond that mountain ranges loomed hard and harsh, jutting into the sky like mangled fists, twisting their hulks into deformed silhouettes.

Before them stretched the ruins of the city they were to name Lubaantún—the Mayan word for "The City of Fallen Stones."

Mitchell-Hedges shivered as he watched the sky darken over Lubaantún. Ribbons of purple and crimson streaked the sky only to vanish in the still of the Mayan twilight. The hush of death, Mitchell-Hedges thought. And he let his mind somersault back through time. He saw the citadel now as an enormous city, with armed soldiers, richly robed priests and great crowds jammed into the huge amphitheater. Children were laughing and eagerly playing games with each other. Lovers strolled through the city arm in arm.

And then the movie ended. And he remembered what was left of the great civilization: the Maya Kekchi Indians living with disease and poverty. Was it a fatal laziness that caused their decline? Had their lives become an unbearable burden? No matter. It was all gone now. The Maya were no longer a great civilization. Mitchell-Hedges shook his head sadly.

A flash of sheet lightning fractured the evening sky. The voices of crickets and frogs, the cries of night birds and jungle animals broke his reverie. Sadly he got to his feet and stepped down from the great pyramid and made his way back to camp.

By 1926 they had only begun to excavate Lubaantún. It covered an area of six square miles and in the center stood a mighty citadel with pyramids, terraces, mounds, walls, houses, subterranean chambers and, most magnificent of all, a huge amphitheater designed to hold more than ten thousand people and approached by two great stairways. The citadel was built over seven and a half acres and originally every foot had been covered with cut white stone and hard cement. Lubaantún had been raised above the level of the jungle, and when it was young must have stood out like a magical pearllike city. The huts of the commoners encircled the perimeter and beyond that acres of what must have been maize had been cultivated to support the populace. Mitchell-Hedges reported that Lubaantún was the "largest single aboriginal structure yet discovered on the American continent."[13]

Lubaantún occupied a gradually sloping ridge, running from north to south and descending to a point a few hundred yards from the Río Colombia, a branch of the

Río Grande. The soil is fertile and freshwater mollusks abound in the navigable waterways. Trade was bartered with the beans of the cacao tree, not only used in the manufacture of chocolate but as the currency of pre-Columbian Middle America. And more recently, Charles Wright of the United Nations Food and Agriculture Organization found that Lubaantún stood in the middle of all the top-quality soil for cacao tree cultivation in all of southern British Honduras.

Many figurines, pottery and stone implements were uncovered and shipped to the museums in Great Britain. And in 1926 Anna joined them. It would be their last visit but their most important. Early the next year, as Anna and her father were in the ruins of a temple, trying to move a heavy wall which had fallen on an altar, they saw an object glisten in the dust.

The crystal skull was buried beneath that altar and three months later the matching jawbone was discovered twenty-five feet away. Lubaantún had given up the skull but kept its secrets to herself.

THE LURE OF ATLANTIS

THE IDEA of lost cities and even continents strikes a responsive chord in all of us, although the response is strongest in those who dwell at the gates of the occult. Yet even if there were proof that such continents as Atlantis and Lemuria once existed and harbored advanced cultures, the impact of this information on our society would be about the same as if it were at last confirmed that intelligent life exists elsewhere in the universe.

Our religious beliefs, morals and social values might have to be reassessed, but life for the great masses of people would go on as usual.

Would it be possible for a supercivilization to exist—one capable of manufacturing a crystal skull—and then disappear without leaving behind any sign of its presence?

Reason, of course, tells us no. That is all too magical. But man is truly a magic animal and knows that science is not an infallible prophet. The bewildering postulations of science itself give the lie to the view that man has already achieved a foothold in the realm of the possible. Less than a century ago, the director of the United States Patent Office resigned his post because he believed that there was nothing left to invent.

The legends of Atlantis* and its sister in the Pacific, Lemuria,† persist and multiply. The subject is finally exhausted and then, when we have closed the door on this intruder forever, a spade turns, a find is made, and the specter of ancient civilizations once again begins to haunt us.

Men who have stepped beyond the bounds of rational inquiry in search for miracle worlds have shown us throughout history that the "real" world often grows to encompass their visions. Writers and philosophers, scientists and poets—many of them intrigued and not a few obsessed with the arcane and the promise of a fuller life in the mysteries of this old earth—have told us of lost worlds filled with marble cathedrals and golden ships. They have envisioned iron floating in the air and a race of

---

* According to L. Sprague and Catherine de Camp in *Ancient Ruins and Archaeology*, "the concept of a land submerged by the sea comes from the earthquake wave that inundated the little Greek island of Atlanta in 426 B.C., the year after Plato was born. The name 'Atlantis' is derived from the same source."

† Lemuria is from the writings of Phillip Lutley Sclater, a British zoologist who had proposed the possibility of a land bridge between Southeast Asia and Madagascar. He noted that tiny, monkeylike animals named lemurs were found chiefly in both places.

blue people walking continents now gone. They have asked us to believe in eternal ice and astral jellyfish. Oddballs! Was Mitchell-Hedges such a man?

Undoubtedly, Mitchell-Hedges had read of Plato's brief description of Atlantis in two of his dialogues, *Timaeus* and *Critias*, written four hundred years before the birth of Christ. In these remarkable dialogues, Plato describes a gigantic island kingdom, with special attention to its wealth and politics, philosophy and religious beliefs.

Although most have considered Plato's tale a political-sociological allegory, to the romantics and the faithful it was the opening refrain of a beautiful Atlantean concert which was to play for twenty-five hundred years and generate countless articles and books, as well as several motion pictures. Atlantis has been located in Antarctica, in North and South Africa, all over the Americas, under the Sahara Desert, in Palestine, in Mexico, and thirteen thousand feet high in the Andes.

At any rate, the island which Plato described and dated as nine thousand years before the time of Solon has remained with us in and out of history. Earlier writings seem to ignore the subject, and no references to Atlantis have ever been found in Hebrew, Roman, Egyptian, or Babylonian histories. This, despite the fact that Critias traces his account to Egyptian sources, confirmed by Solon—who even took great pains, supposedly, to explain that the Greek names for the places and kings of Atlantis were only necessary translations from the original sources. But, repeatedly, the Atlantean legends return to knock at the doors of our imagination. During the Middle Ages, stories and tales of a vast continent somewhere in the oceans to the west became commonplace, and with the dawn of the Renaissance and physical exploration, maps and charts were sprinkled with islands and lands both real and imagined.

Stories came back to Europe of physically terrifying, baffling places, shrouded in mist and fog, where mysterious lights and shadows danced to an unearthly rhythm, and brightly robed priests, magicians, and even black rabbits walked the land at midnight. Others talked of monsters and giants, six-fingered women and cyclopean men. The literature was both obscure and entertaining, but it lacked the touch of documented fact that could make it palatable to us today.

When the University of Athens dispatched an archaeological search party in 1967 for yet another try at proving the existence of Atlantis, a full century of such attempts was rounded out. It was in 1868 that the remarkable adventurer and romanticist Heinrich Schliemann turned his first shovelful of earth in Asia Minor. The object of his immediate quest was the "topless towers of Ilium," the Troy of Homer. But his uncanny success convinced succeeding generations that a more exotic prize, the fabled Atlantis, was only another excavation away.

We now speak of Schliemann as the great German archaeologist, discoverer of Troy and Mycenae, but in the middle of the last century he was little more than an amateur treasure hunter. As a matter of fact, Schliemann had been an American citizen ever since a visit to the California gold fields in 1850. Before that he had garnered a small fortune for himself in Russia during the Crimean War. Homer's *Iliad* and *Odyssey* had been read to him as a child. These heroic legends were considered about as historical as Aesop's fables or the story of the birth of Venus. But while Schliemann amassed his wealth he maintained a secret dream of one day verifying his boyhood fantasies. He would dig up the walls that were breached only by that first of Grecian gifts, a wooden horse.

Schliemann's childhood faith, persistence, and showmanship were rewarded almost immediately, and not only by worldwide fame but by academic honors and undreamed-of treasure. His archaeology was less than scientific, and later had to be buttressed with the expertise of university scholars. Yet almost singlehanded he had uncovered evidence of a vast pre-Hellenic civilization that had gone unheralded in scientific circles for more than two millennia.

The tone of Schliemann's work on Mycenae and Troy was captured by such authors as Lewis Spence and H. S. Bellamy, writing on the subject of Atlantis. Both wrote in the scholarly tradition. But the public was captivated by extravagant hopes of new revelations of lost civilizations. Why should the offhand stories of Atlantis be considered less reliable than the fables of Homer? The former was prose; the latter was poetry.

"There are armchair scientists who have scoffed but had they dug on the floors of the caves with us they

would have changed their minds and revised their ideas,"
Mitchell-Hedges wrote. "Those who deny that Atlantis
ever existed outside the fertile imagination of some early
writers claim in support of their denials the fact that no
evidence had been found to justify a theory that a highly
civilized people existed anywhere on earth before 6000
B.C. . . . Now the evidence has been found."[14]

With that, Mitchell-Hedges zeroed in and pointed out
there was a likely outpost of Atlantis within the Bay
Islands off the coast of Honduras. The artifacts which
his expedition uncovered displayed an astounding quality
of workmanship and detail.

He was convinced of the existence of Atlantis and
believed that they had reached a high degree of culture
thousands of years before our recorded history. He equated
the theories of the Great Flood with the destruction of
the continent and postulated that any survivors were probably the precursors of the Mayan civilization.

The *New York American* reported his conclusions regarding the origin of the races in Central America. He
wrote that great civilizations with a population in the
millions existed long before the Christian era began. These
people were

> possessed of a high culture, a knowledge and stage of
> government regarding which today there is a blank
> chapter in the history of science.
>   Much time, money and scientific research have been
> devoted to exploration and investigation of the great

Maya cities in Yucatán, but these are comparatively modern. Then we have the more ancient Maya ruins— Copan, for example, in the republic of Honduras, Lubaantún in British Honduras, and others which belong to that period known as the First Empire.

For years science has grappled with that fascinating problem—the origin of the Maya, the greatest aboriginal civilization the world has ever known—but between November 10, 752 B.C. and August 6, 613 B.C., as reckoned by our present calendar, all knowledge of it ends. At that remote period the Mayas had an extremely high culture; their sculpturing was remarkable, comparing favorably with that of ancient Greece and the best of our present day.

They were proficient in the production of beautiful paintings on stucco, and their mosaic work has never been excelled. Their buildings were a wonderful achievement and even compared with our modern ideas and standards would be regarded with admiration.

One could not have a better example than the immense citadel of Lubaantún in British Honduras, which Dr. Thomas Gann and I discovered in 1924. Here we found one building in the erection of which millions of blocks of cut stone were employed, and which covers EIGHT ACRES.

Within, and actually a part of this edifice, are solid stone pyramids, while across the top and in the center runs a Via Sacra constructed of cement.

This road terminates in a great stone stairway, over one hundred and fifty feet wide, leading down to an amphitheater, surrounded by terraces and flat-topped pyramids, with seating accommodation for thousands.[15]

In that and a subsequent article for the *New York American*, Mitchell-Hedges continued his speculations on the similarities of the Old and New Worlds:

"There are similarities between these objects and the existing archeological evidence through study of which science reads the distant 'pre-history' past of the Old World.

"This newly discovered culture ante-dated Egypt's beginnings by many thousands of years—perhaps tens of thousands.

"I hesitate to estimate the antiquity of this civilization. My own 'speculations'—I label them as such, although there exist certain bases for computation—lead to a belief that this civilization flourished certainly not later than 15,000 B.C., or that possibly it dates BEYOND 25,000 B.C."[16]

Off the Bay Islands, Mitchell-Hedges pulled many pre-Flood remnants and excavated twenty-one sites in the five tiny islands. Mitchell-Hedges was careful to note that in some cases the stone faces were anthropologically similar to the Central American Indian while others were crafted with the high cheekbone and aquiline nose of the North American Indian.

Upon the island of Bonaca he discovered an eight-hundred-yard mound wall enclosure, the top of which was paved with flat stones. In this place of worship he discovered two immense monoliths which, he noted, were similar to stone formations at Stonehenge. The stones measured almost 7 feet in height and 2½ feet through the base.

He also unearthed well-proportioned vases, objects of copper and bronze, and found upon a hilltop a huge hewn stone with strange markings upon it. There was no known mechanism that could have moved it to this remote pinnacle.

In the hastily abandoned chambers, among the awe-inspiring evidence of nature's upheaval, he discovered oddly carved stones and weird figurines of grotesque animals and reptiles, which, he surmised, might once have roamed the earth. But out of all these artifacts not one had any relation to the culture of the Maya, Aztec, Toltec or to other cultures of the area.

On a slope that was once terraced downward to the sea he found a specimen in the form of an animal. It was about four inches long and pierced with round holes. Another similar object was also found in the form of a man. It appeared at first to be a solid piece of stone but upon closer examination he found it packed with dirt. Subsequent cleaning proved it to be a simple wind instrument—perhaps the original ocarina.

It must have been an eerie experience to experiment with those instruments—unplayed for centuries.

The authenticity of the Mitchell-Hedges finds received wide endorsement. George C. Heye, Director of the Heye Foundation at the Museum of the American Indian in New York, wrote, "Your own observations, and the United States Government surveys in Nicaragua, prove conclusively that at some remote period a tremendous earth movement of cataclysmic force must have taken

place in that part of the world . . . and that your excavations have actually unearthed the cultural artifacts of
a prehistoric people that existed prior to the great earth
movement . . . your discoveries open up an entirely new
vista in regard to the ancient civilizations of the American
continent."[17]

In reading through the more detailed reports of the
Mitchell-Hedges expedition, one cannot help but believe
that he had unearthed a civilization hitherto unknown.

A lot of explaining remains to be done about the similarities of the civilizations of Egypt and the Yucatán.
Modern-day archaeologists—like their brethren in other
scientific disciplines—tend to take themselves quite seri-
ously. With few exceptions, scholars and teachers have
always been quick to disassociate themselves from ideas
not accepted by the scientific establishment. How can we
be so certain, therefore, that our globe does not still
conceal the evidences of civilizations beyond our memory
and produce such objects as the crystal skull?

How can we be satisfied that adequate and objective
research has probed the ruins of the Mayas for their full
implications? Science by its very nature tends to favor
what can be proved as against data that lead to further
mysteries. "There is not one shred of evidence to support
the theory of past and unknown civilizations," the skeptics
chant. But the Mayan civilization has simply been put in a
neat niche by the establishment. With only 5 per cent or
less of the ruins in the Yucatán uncovered, archaeologists

have concluded that this civilization was built without the aid of the wheel.

There is a scientific limbo reserved for such realities as the Mayan ruins. After a period of purification, a few facts advance to the textbook level. Thus far, this process has been slow indeed. Until some relationship is discovered without sanctified theories, the Mayan mystery will remain just that.

Like the underground waterways that flow beneath their country, the Mayan civilization works in enigmatic tunnels through our rationalizations. The Mayas had no work animals and no domestic animals, no wagons or carts; yet they built enormous monuments, temples, and cities—and pyramids. Much information has been lost concerning their civilization partly because the Bishop of Yucatán, Diego de Landa, in 1566 had almost every Mayan document he could find destroyed as the work of Satan. Certain extant books, such as the *Chilam Balam,* are filled with historical inaccuracies and unpardonable mistakes. What are we to believe?

The Mayas built with mathematical accuracy; their sculpture and friezes related to particular dates. Obsessed with the passing of time, the Mayas wove the symbols of days and months into their architecture. Yet today, even with dating techniques currently available, it is practically impossible to chronicle their history because we lack a point of temporal reference.

Yet the calendar we use is Mayan. After tedious calculations, we have finally put the duration of the solar year at 365.242127 days. The Mayas had calculated it as 365.24219. The figure was arrived at using techniques completely unknown to us.

The observatory at Chichén Itzá gave the Mayan observers an incredible knowledge of the universe and the cosmos. It was a far better observatory than the European society had constructed as late as the seventeenth century. To this day, there is a two-week discrepancy in the records of George Washington's birthday because the Gregorian calendar, which corrected centuries of drift in the European calendar, was not universally accepted.

Similarities between the ancient peoples of Mexico and of Egypt cannot be ignored. Did the civilizations spring up simultaneously, or spread from one region to the other? What possessed these people to build without the wheel?

Travel ninety miles north of Mexico City and witness the Pyramids of the Sun and Moon at Teotihuacán. Climb these structures, and there, spread out before you, are the cities of the Toltecs. Visions can be conjured up with a minimum of tequila, and the fields come alive with a blaze of color and the magic of past centuries. The Pyramid of the Sun is twice as large as the Pyramid of Cheops. We are curious and pass on. Hidden deep within the jungle are secrets yet to be uncovered. Some, like the crystal skull, have already been discounted by the Age of Discovery.

But since the finding of the crystal skull, what has been done about the ruins of Lubaantún? In January of 1970,

a team of British scientists and archaeologists headed by
Norman Hammond, a research fellow of the Centre of
Latin American Studies at Cambridge, took up residence
in the Lubaantún ruins in the hope of establishing some
sort of cultural sequence. The expedition was under the
sponsorship of Cambridge and the Peabody Museum of
Archaeology and Ethnology of Harvard University.

Two months later one totally unexpected conclusion
emerged with startling clarity. It was the fact that not
only did the spectacular architecture of Lubaantún date
from the end of the classic Maya civilization, but the
foundation for the first settlement there took place only
shortly before. That would place it early in the eighth
century A.D.

But an explanation may be offered for this. Thirty miles
across the jungle to the southwest and within a few miles
of the Guatemalan frontier is the site of Pusilhà. Pusilhà
is the only other known religious center in that part of the
Maya lowlands and was linked to Lubaantún along the
edge of the mountains by natural trade routes.

Dates on the monuments show they were erected between 573 A.D. and 731 A.D., and after the later date it is
possible that Pusilhà ceased to exist as a religious center.
Hammond thinks it is possible that about that time the
site of Lubaantún was founded. If these findings are accurate it is quite possible that the major ceremonial center
for that part of the southeastern lowlands was actually
moved from Pusilhà to Lubaantún late in the first half of
the eighth century A.D.

If Hammond is correct in these initial findings, it means

in all probability that the crystal skull had to be taken to Lubaantún after its construction as a religious citadel. Why it was left when the site was abandoned we shall never know. Then too, we are reluctantly condemned to acknowledge the possibility it was taken to Lubaantún by none other than F. A. Mitchell-Hedges.

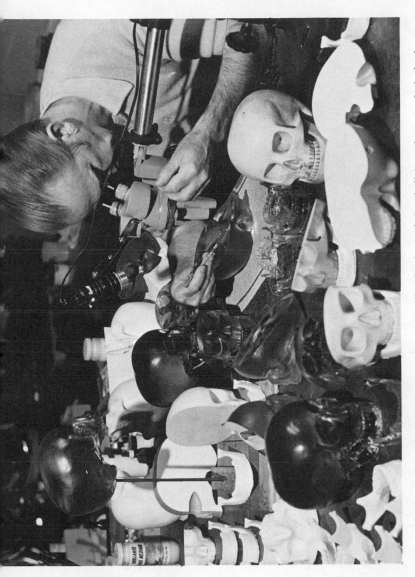

(PHOTO 1) Frank Dorland at work in his studio. Castings of the skull have been made in both plaster and epoxies. Cross sections were then cut, studied and measured.

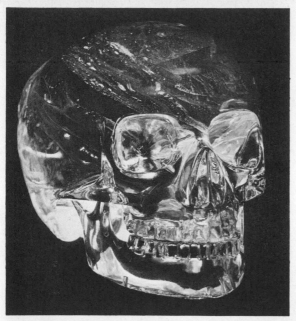

(PHOTO 2) A ¾ view of the Mitchell-Hedges skull.

(PHOTO 3) Front view of the Mitchell-Hedges skull. Note the almost perfect bilateral symmetry of the carving.

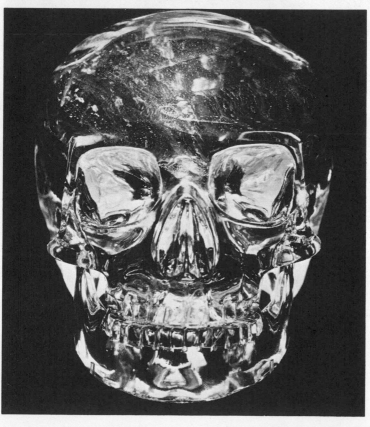

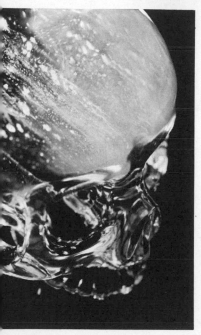

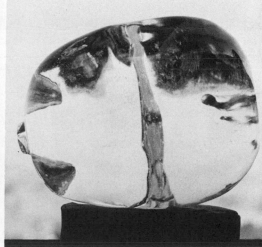

(PHOTO 4) Side view of the Mitchell-Hedges skull with the jawbone detached.

(PHOTO 5) Photograph of the skull showing the relieved zygomatic arches which act as "light pipes" to channel illumination from the base of the skull into tiny concave lenses in the eye sockets.

(PHOTO 6) Top view of the cranium. Note the reflection of the ribbon prism carved into the base of the skull and the absence of any suture marks. The prism also acts as a magnifier.

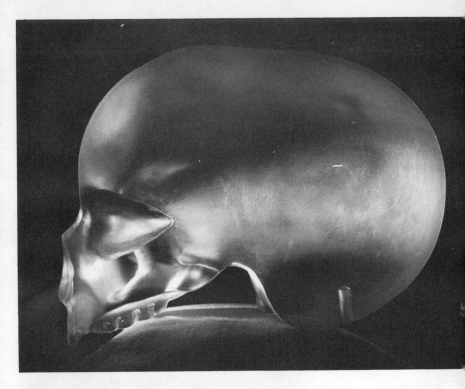

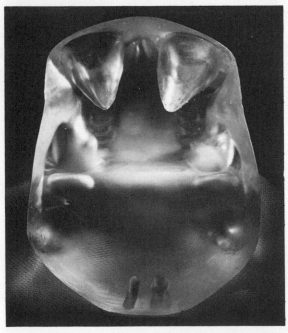

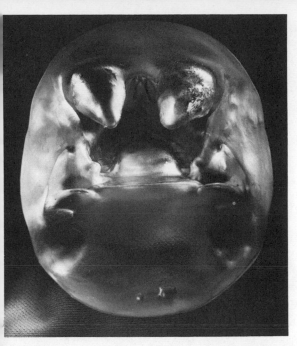

(PHOTOS 7–10) Cross sections of the skull cast in epoxy to display the exact symmetry of the orbital excavations. Note the cylindrical protrusions into the base of the cranium. These tiny excavations were probably meant to receive weighted rods to serve as counterweights to enable the skull to "talk."

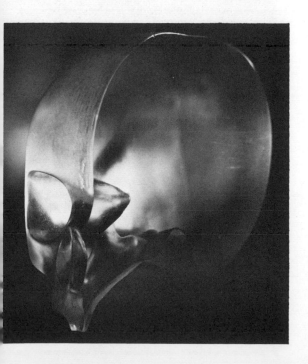

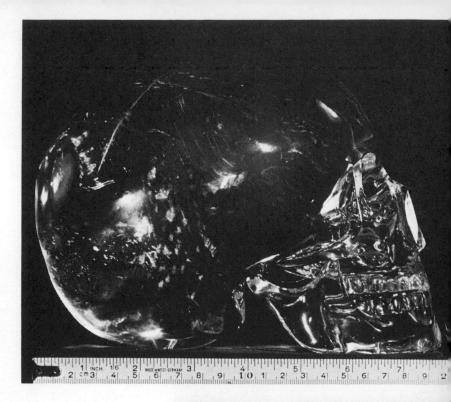

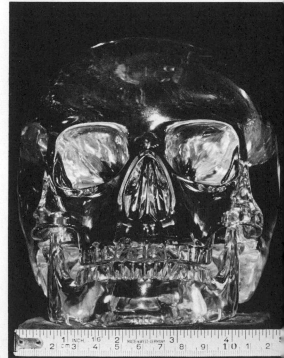

(PHOTOS 11–12) *Left:* Side and front views of the skull with scale.

(PHOTO 13) *Below:* A skull of crystal half the size of the Mitchell-Hedges skull. It has been classified as Aztec in origin and was probably the ornament at the end of a staff. It is now in the *Musée de l'homme* in Paris.

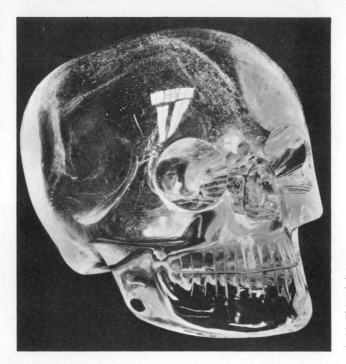

(PHOTO 14) The British Museum crystal skull, which was discovered in Mexico in 1889. It has been classified as pre-Columbian, probabl[y] Aztec or Mixtec.

(PHOTO 15) The British Museum specimen and the Mitchell-Hedges skull side b[y] side. Measurements between the two are almost identical. The Mitchell-Hedge[s] specimen is much more refined and detailed. Some authorities believe the Britis[h] specimen is an "unfinished" version or "blank" of the Mitchell-Hedges skull. Th[e] teeth are not sculptured in any degree and no effort was made to excavate th[e] zygomatic arches or relieve the jawbone.

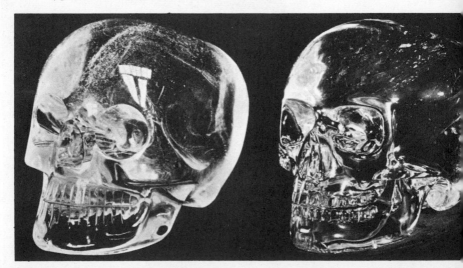

(PHOTO 16) F. A. Mitchell-Hedges.

(PHOTO 17) Anna Le Guillon Mitchell-Hedges.

(PHOTO 18) *Top right:* Farley Castle, owned and occupied by F. A. Mitchell-Hedges. It dates from the early seventeenth century and is said to have been built for Simon the Red, King of the Gypsies. The castle contained thousands of treasures.

(PHOTO 19) *Right:* Mitchell-Hedges, Lady Richmond Brown and Dr. Thomas Gann at Lubaantún.

(PHOTO 20) Lady Richmond Brown with Bantanecos Indian women.

(PHOTO 21) Excavating the side of the Great Pyramid at Lubaantún.

(PHOTO 22) Part of the South Grandstand or tier of stone seats at Lubaantún.

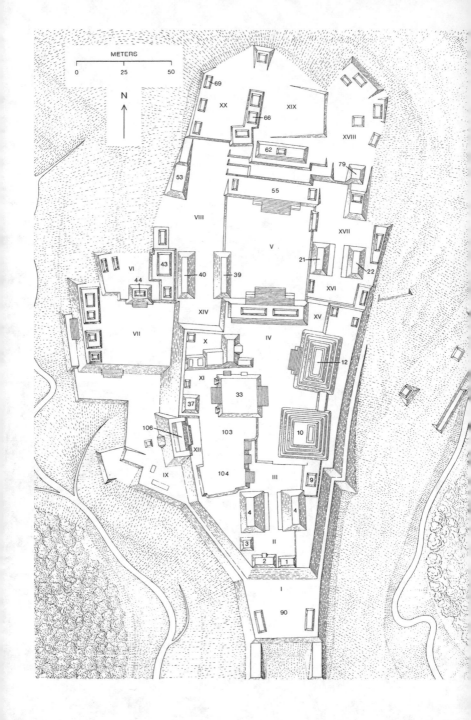

(PHOTOS 23–24) Map and reconstruction at Lubaantún. Dr. Thomas Gann, who accompanied Mitchell-Hedges, found it "absolutely unique on the American continent." It covered seven and one-half acres, all of which were covered with hard white stone. It presented an extraordinary combination of fortress, theater and religious citadels.

17th February, 1968

Mr. F N Dorland,
Messrs Dorlands,
280 Panoramic Highway,
Mill Valley.
California.94943

The Rock Crystal Skull first appeared
during our expedition to Lubaantum in 1926.
We went during 1926, and left before the rainy
season in 1927.

We found the building, and were digging
in the temple, moving a heavy wall which had
fallen on the altar. This took some time
because the rocks were so heavy we could only
move about 6 a day and left completely
exhausted.

I came upon the Skull buried beneath the
altar, but it was some three months later
before the jaw was found which was about
25 feet away.

On this expedition ws:

Father   (dec)
Myself
Jane Houlson (dec) Father's secretary.
Capt. Joyce (dec) British Museum
Dr. Gann
Lady Richmond Brown (dec)

                    A Mitchell-Hedges

(sgd)

(PHOTO 25) An affidavit signed by Anna Mitchell-Hedges attesting to
the authenticity of the find.

Atlantis Was No Myth but the Cradle Of American Races, Declares Hedges

AMAZING—Explorer Hedges (right) examining some astounding discoveries in the "Cradle of Civilization:" human heads reduced to fist size. Left, petrified stone head, once the wooden top of Chiefstick with skull showing same formation as that of the American Indian.

Excavations of Twenty-one Sites on Five Caribbean Islands Confirm His Theory of Pre-Flood Cataclysm, Says Noted Explorer

By F. A. MITCHELL-HEDGES,
Famous Explorer, F. Z. S., F. L. S., F. R. G. S., F. R. A. I., F. E. S., Member of the Maya Committee of the British Museum.

MANY weirdly strange mysteries are explained by discovery of evidences of the world's oldest known culture —a pre-Flood civilization—in the Bay Islands, off the coast of Honduras.

The most isolated primitive Indian tribes —I have lived among twenty—retain ancient rituals from some dim past:

A "Feast to the God of Fertility"; it is the Old World "Harvest Festival." A "wailing ceremony" for the dead: here we

the arts, in music, in sculpturing; workers in metal and masters of certain sciences, including medicine and astronomy, the latter, of course, implying mathematical ability. I am convinced, moreover, that they were masters in what we might term the Social sciences; that they had developed, through religion, government and traditional folk-customs, a racial stability and security which we may well envy them today.

American Races Born in Atlantis

They were, perhaps, not advanced—as we would conceive it—in the modern mechanics

(PHOTOS 26–28) Mitchell-Hedges made headlines in the *New York American* during the early 1930s.

CENTRAL AMERICA IS ONE OF THE CRADLES OF MANKIND,' DECLARES MITCHELL-HEDGES

Vast Cities of Antiquity Hitherto Unsuspected Lie Buried in Tropical Jungles'

By F. A. MITCHELL-HEDGES,
F.R.G.S., F.Z.S., F.R.A.I., F.A.G.S.

In previous articles of this series, F. A. Mitchell-Hedges, internationally noted as an explorer, has described the discovery of amazing prehistoric relics and evidences of a civilization of undreamed antiquity in Honduras, in Central America. A new expedition, headed by himself and Lady Richmond Brown, is now accompanying himself and Lady Richmond Brown. Mr. Mitchell-Hedges here accumulates factual regarding the aboriginal races of Central America, based on his recent explorations and other researches he has made over a number of years in that region.

I believe one of the cradles of mankind to have been Central America; that the entire scientific conception of the aboriginal races of Central America and a large portion of South America will have to be revised.

Basing my conclusions upon the recent discoveries of prehistoric ruins and relics made in Honduras by the expedition led by myself, as well as upon our earlier explorations, I am convinced that still lying buried in the jungles of that part of the world are the remains of cities of an antiquity hitherto unsuspected.

I am certain that future exploration work will reveal definite evidence of a great civilization with a population numbering millions, which existed long before the Christian era.

My conviction is that these people were possessed of a knowledge of science and state of government in some cases superior to our own today there is a blank chapter in the book of science.

That the arts, money and scientific research have been developed to exploration and investigation of the great Maya cities in Yucatan, but these have been mostly ruins of Maya temples. They are no more applicable to the ruins of Copan, for example, in the republic of Honduras, than to Mayan cities which belong to that period

PREHISTORIC—A noble urn, measuring more than three feet in circumference, excavated by the Mitchell-Hedges-Richmond Brown expedition in Honduras. Below, Mr. Mitchell-Hedges and a companion examining some of the immense finds of the American Indian in New York. Scientists declare Maya an immense age, of a period far antedating the Christian era.
—Above, Courtesy of the Museum of the American Indian, Heye Foundation.

DELVING INTO THE PAST—F. A. Mitchell-Hedges, Lady Richmond Brown and Mr. Karl Stein examining some of the

The procession of the equinoxes was well known to them; they could predict with accuracy eclipses, and solve the most difficult astronomical problems. This is what science has discovered they actually did, and proves the profound brain power of these Christian era peoples. It is also significant that the Mayas were the first people in the world to invent a symbol for zero.

One thing is certain, the Mayas, like the original Americans, built up a great start, thickly populated and of splendid civilization, and this one is forced to the question: How long must it have taken these men to acquire

remain today almost as perfect as at that remote period. The Mayas attained a form of government and an astronomical and mathematical knowledge that would be envied by our world today.

For example, one of their time units was 374 years, another, a vast period so immense that it even makes other set periods. They created a calendar system which started on a date synchronizing with our 14th of October, 3373 B.C., no fewer than five pre-set figures. The Maya calendar

knowledge whatever and no even the animal sense to feed themselves properly.

But against this there are certain tribes, such as the remnant tribes, the present Romanze Indians, who still preserve, as evidence, by their intricate picture writing on cloth, and also of the reduced human heads and bodies can be seen at the remnant Incasle culture in the dim past.

Again there are the Jivaros and Tsolola Indians of Ecuador, who today are still able, as the result of a very high scientific knowledge, to reduce after death, human heads, preserving both the epidermis and the countenance, perfectly—a form of mummifi-

priceless relics of a vanished race which they found during their recent explorations of aboriginal ruins in Honduras.
—International Newsreel Photo

has been handed down to them through countless generations and is an illustration of the great scientific knowledge they once must

Examples of the picture-writing on cloth, and also of the reduced human heads and bodies can be seen at the Museum of the American Indian in New York [Heye Foundation].

It is suggested that all these different cultures existed within a widely defined area, and located themselves in Central America! People do not evolve synthetically from the common. We may, therefore, did these tribes originate?

Weird
Indian Mastered Secret of Mummifying Process

But assume that the Maya migrated in such a manner, this leaves entirely unaccounted for the large mass of Indians still living today,

might well be that the Maya and many other Indian races which exist were at a remote period one vast civilization with their genesis in Central America.

One thing is certain—long before the Christian era the jungles and swamps which today cover this mysterious country did not exist. The land was crop-bearing and fertile, and had to be to feed its immense population.

has been handed down to them through countless generations and is an illustration of the great scientific knowledge they once must

was densely populated, a mighty civilization.

Even more, I think today I have the proofs of an earth convulsion beneath which the earthquakes recorded, thru the last few centuries were mere tremors. And as a result, the configuration of the land in that part of the world, possibly thousands of years ago, was changed completely to what is today.

The more one delves into the riddle of the Maya. Comparing modern-day more intriguing America—the more baffling and fascinating does it become.

Consider what these aboriginal races have given us as an example. Like the Maya as maize, the common rubber potatoes, tobacco, quinine, cotton, and indeed nearly all our valuable food products were bequeathed by this wonderful civilization to the world.

Populous
Scores of Ancient Cities Buried in Honduras

In fact, in peopling was the need for arable land that every hill and mountainside was spread on artificial terraces, even to make the teeming masses that inhabited this part of the world.

Take Chichen Itza, which is only one of three more or more Maya cities. Dr. Morley, the eminent Maya authority, awaiting discovery!

Explorer Hedges Finds Pre-Mayan City Buried Beneath Caribbean Sea

THE FIRST OCARINAS—A civilization believed to have existed in islands off the Honduras coast before the flood had developed crude wind musical instruments. At the left, above, are shown large deep note "ocarinas"; the the right, a small treble tone instrument.

RIGHT— F. A. Mitchell-Hedges, British explorer, who has uncovered evidences of a pre-flood civilization off the Honduras coast.

Exquisitely Painted Vases, Prehistoric Musical Instruments and Beads Uncovered in Hastily Abandoned Chambers

By F. A. MITCHELL-HEDGES,

Famous Explorer, P. Z. S., P. L. S., F. R. G. S., F. R. A. I., F. E. S., Member of the Maya Committee of the British Museum.

THE VESTIGES OF a luxurious civilization which flour-

ly painted; curious stone carvings, unknown to science; perfectly modelled pottery figurines

| WILL SHED |

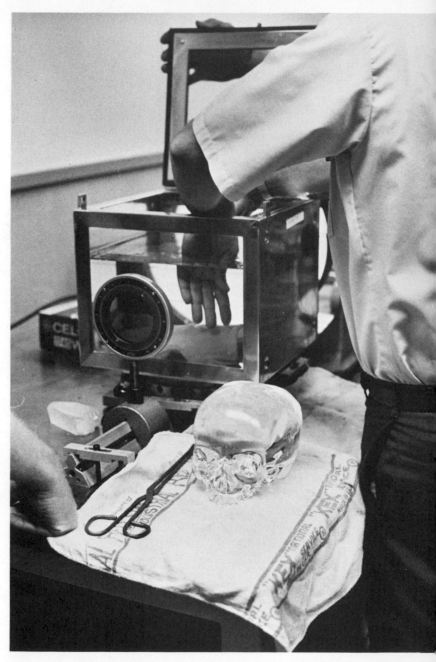

(PHOTO 29) The skull in the laboratories of the Hewlett-Packard Company prior to being tested under polarized light.

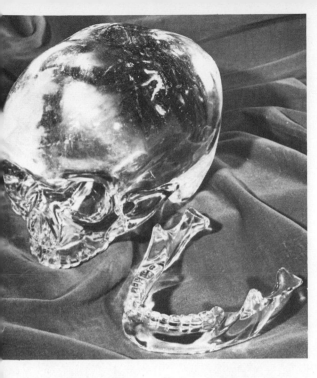

(PHOTO 30) Photo of skull with jawbone detached. The jawbone was the Mayan head-variant element for the number 10. It also enabled Mayan priests to make the skull give the illusion of speaking.

(PHOTO 31) The skull being viewed in a solution of benzyl alcohol. Note it is almost invisible, but a faint portion of the right eye socket is visible.

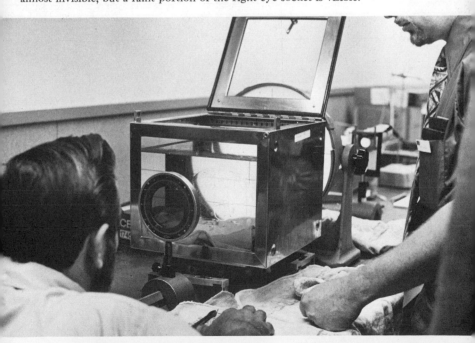

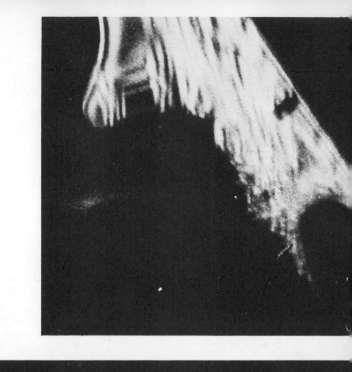

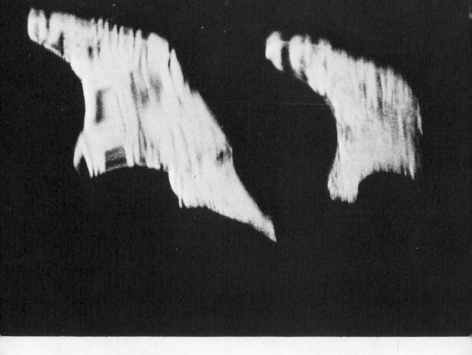

(PHOTOS 32–33) Photographs of the jawbone by polarized light. Note stress marks indicative of "twinning." The jawbone was once attached to the skull itself.

(PHOTO 34) *Below:* One of the various scenes seen in the eye sockets. This one bears an uncanny resemblance to the observatory at Chichén Itzá: the famous Caracol (circled).

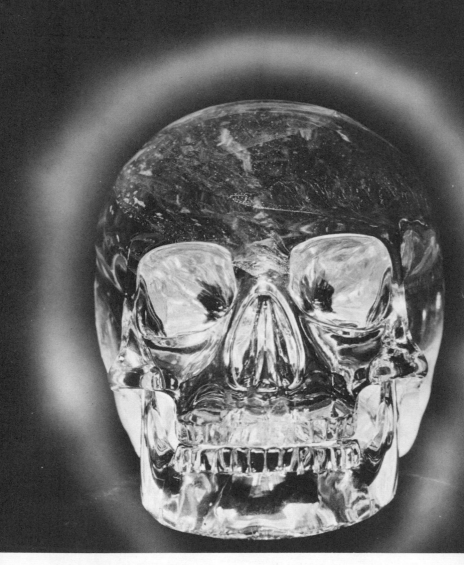

(PHOTO 35) Simulated photograph by Frank Dorland showing the aura Dorland has seen around the skull.

THE SKULL MOTIF AND THE MAYAN DISCOVERY OF TEN

EARLY in man's cultural development, the skull, like the rest of the skeleton, became both a symbolic and thematic element. In early Egyptian art, the use of the skull as a symbol of any sort was virtually nonexistent. It was during the Hellenistic and postclassical periods that the use of the skull as a symbol began to evolve. Since those times, the use of the skull as a death's-head became relatively common. The buccaneer's Jolly Roger is almost identical with the warning on containers of poisons. And as far north as Point Hope, Alaska, tombs of an advanced Arctic culture contained skulls whose empty eye sockets contained carefully carved ivory spheres. A list of the ways the human skull has been portrayed in history would fill volumes.

"It is evident that the cult of the skull or at least skull worship, has been in the past a worldwide practice among ancient peoples," Dorland says. "From the Pacific islands to Tibet, from Egypt to Mexico, skull worship is found in every corner of the globe. And it seems that almost all of this practice held the skull in extremely high esteem. It was worshipped and adored and saved and revered. The symbol of the skull as a gruesome ugly death head, seems to be most common in the last fifteen hundred years.

"The actual quartz skull is a magnificently sophisticated bit of masterful art and it has nothing at all to do with death or mortality in the eyes of its original makers. It was believed to be a godhead—a symbol of all encompassing knowledge and wisdom. I believe it was a fountainhead of power and a magical talisman."

Dorland, in his research, speculates that the Mitchell-Hedges skull could even represent earlier deities. He points out two possibilities: Ea and Mazda.

"Ea was one of the three deities of the Babylonian pantheon and the lord of all wisdom. Mazda was an ancient Iranian god, illuminator of the universe and another likely candidate. I think it logical that Ea and Mazda could possibly be the same god, simply evolving in different areas. Both, for example, were gods of wisdom, both possessed a great and encompassing love of man, and both were great magicians.

"Ea was the god of water and Mazda the god of light. Ea, being the water god, would be sculptured in a material that represents exactly what he was: wisdom and water. The human brain box signifying wisdom and the quartz crystal symbolizing water. It would have been relatively simple to manufacture the skull from gold or silver but it would not be suitable for a water god."

Dorland has been unable to find any other god that would be so suitable to be carved from pure rock quartz.

But nowhere in the world has the skull motif had a greater importance than in the Central American cultures, both modern and pre-Hispanic. In these cultures, the skull motif shows up in an astounding variety of forms. For instance, the center of the Aztec calendar is a fleshless face; the Aztec god Xototl, twin of Quetzalcóatl, had the face of a skull; mosaic inlays of skulls were made by the Nahuas and the skull was an important thematic element in the gold work of the Mixtecs.

In Mexico, the skull is constantly used as an element in ceramics, reliefs and sculptures. It is used in arches and pageantry, crafts, politics, the manufacture of toys; even tiny sugar skulls are a popular confection among the children.

One of the most popular holidays of the year is the Feast of All Saints—the Mexican Halloween. Many reasons have been offered as an explanation for the prevalence of the skull motif in these cultures but none so intriguing as the possibility that the skull could possibly be related to the development of the mathematical concept of zero by the Mayas.

It has been pointed out, notably in *Indian Historian*,

the quarterly publication of the American Indian Historical Society, that the skull motif was closely related to the Maya discovery of zero. The Mayas invented the zero around 200 B.C.—long before the concept evolved in other civilizations. It has further been suggested that the Mitchell-Hedges crystal skull served as the archetype of the Mayan head variant for ten and that the skull was made as a sort of standard for the concept.[18]

Around a thousand years before the early Hindu civilization was credited with the development of the concept of zero, this idea was already firmly planted in the intellects of the high Maya priests. Further, this mathematical concept did not reach Western Europe until the Middle Ages—centuries after its development in the Western Hemisphere.

The possibility that Thor Hyerdahl suggests—that man traveled westward across the Pacific—might well explain the expansion of this concept from a South American culture to a civilization of the East.

At any rate, there is little quarrel among authorities that sometime around 200 B.C. the Mayan concept of zero was developed. And as the late authority on the ancient Maya, Sylvanus G. Morley, commented, they developed man's first positional arithmetical system, one involving the concept of zero "which even today stands as one of the brilliant achievements of the human mind."[19]

In what way, however, does the concept of a skull with a detachable jawbone and the prevalence of the skull symbolism in South American cultures have to do with

mathematics? The answer probably lies in the fact that
the Mayan system of notation is based on the number
twenty (vigesimal) rather than by tens in our decimal
system. And just as we use both Roman* and Arabic
numerals, two sets of symbols were used by that culture,
both employing the concept of zero.

One is known as the "normal form," a system of bar
and dot numerals in which a dot has the value of one
and the bar a value of five. In various combinations the
numbers from one to nineteen could be written. Zero in
this system is symbolized by the glyph of a shell.

The other method of numerical notation is usually
referred to as the "head variant" system and uses the

* The concept of zero is lacking in this notation. To reach the
number of nineteen using the symbols of I, V and X, a subtractive
process must be employed. The dot-bar system of the Mayas requires
but simple addition.

head symbols of deities to represent the numbers from zero to thirteen. But most significant is that this system utilized the symbol of the detached skeletal jawbone to represent the number ten. Thus if the fleshless jawbone were added to the head variant figure for seven, the number would automatically become seventeen. This is an amazing concept considering the age in which this was discovered—equaling or perhaps even outstripping the contributions of a Pythagoras, a Euclid or an Archimedes.

Was it a mere accident that the jawbone of a skeleton was chosen to represent such an important mathematical concept? Certainly a less macabre symbol could have been employed. But symbolism of the most basic themes were used throughout the culture—a culture which recognized the head as the brain box and the carrier of intellect and rationality. What symbol of the human anatomy, stripped of all its fleshly characteristics, could serve better as the archetype of man's intellectual potential? And so the selection was accepted, probably was passed into law and became the most important mathematical symbol ever to develop in this culture.

The use of the skull and its detached jawbone, it may be concluded, would make maximum effective use of the symbolism that employed the concept of zero. The symbol was constantly kept before the eyes of the people in their day-to-day existence by its ubiquitousness in erected stelae, friezes and other artifacts.

It is within the realm of possibility that the Mitchell-

Hedges skull was the "platinum yardstick" for the head variant idea of the Mayan concept of zero. It would have also served the double purpose of a speculum—a device for focusing on a fixed point for religious and metaphysical purposes.

The reason for this idea, of course, is the lack of suture marks on the skull itself, which would impede the scryer's access into the elsewhere world of crystallomancy.

The British Museum specimen may well have been a copy for safekeeping in the event that the more refined model was lost or destroyed. That was probably exactly what happened. Before Cortez, the latter empire of the Mayas was rife with civil war—a conflict so extreme that even the Aztecs were enlisted as mercenaries. Eventually the Aztecs looted the Mayan treasure house of valuable religious objects.

Therefore, it is entirely possible that the bounty of this loot was hauled out of Mexico by an officer of Maximilian's army and became the skull now in residence at the British Museum.

If these arguments are correct, it becomes increasingly important to take note of the fact that the Mitchell-Hedges jawbone—the Mayan symbol of ten—was separate. And was it indeed part of the original crystal and detached at a later date? Where did the Mayas get the skull in the first place? Was it indeed left to them by an earlier, now forgotten civilization? Morever, was the crystal skull itself the very reason for the emergence and preponderance of the skull motif throughout these cultures?

○◎○◎○◎○◎○◎○◎○◎○◎○◎○◎○◎○◎○◎○◎○◎○

eight

WHAT IT IS

THE MITCHELL-HEDGES SKULL, it will be recalled, is a giant hunk of quartz crystal, clear and flawed by en-capulated bubbles and "veins" common to the material.

Quartz crystal is one of the earth's most prevalent and most beautiful formations,* and is an important constit-uent of other rocks such as granite, many gneisses and crystalline schists. In fact; there are so many varieties of crystal that only the most knowledgeable expert can iden-tify them all.

It is an extremely hard substance and rates on the Mohs' scale at a hardness factor of 7, which means it cannot be scratched by a knife (on the same scale, diamonds are

---

* The word "crystal" is from the Greek *crystallos*, or "clear ice." The name "quartz" was first used by Georgius Agricola in 1530 and is an old German word of uncertain origin.

rated at 10). The specific gravity is 2.65. Typical of quartz crystal is a hexagonal prism terminated at the ends by six faces in the shape of acute isosceles triangles. The color of crystal varies widely from purple to pink, green to brown, to nearly black. Quartz is abundant and inexpensive although specimens of clear white quartz the size of a human head are unusual. In addition, the supply of quartz suitable for advanced electronic applications have led to the technology of "growing" synthetic quartz for these needs. It is a nonconductor of electricity and is insusceptible to acids except hydrofluoric.

The phenomenon known as the piezoelectric effect is common to quartz crystal. This effect occurs when pressure or tensile stress is applied to the crystal, and develops a positive and negative charge on alternate prism edges. For this and other reasons, quartz is used for frequency control in broadcasting stations, electronic oscillators and frequency time standards. Today, quartz crystal oscillators remain the workhorses of virtually every frequency control application. In such applications, a quartz resonator (which is a quarter-sized slice of crystal) is mounted between conducting electrodes coated with a thin deposit of a metallic substance, usually gold. An alternating voltage in a selected natural frequency causes it to vibrate at an extremely constant rate. The crystal resonator itself behaves as if it were an electrical network and it imposes its own frequency on the oscillating circuit.

Quartz grows in a spiral and for reasons not fully understood inclines toward a certain direction. Thus, crystals can be either right- or left-handed in a crystallographic sense, depending upon the conditions of their growth. It is also possible for several crystals of the same and even different types to twin and intergrow. Crystals which have twinned are quite common. Under a sharp impact twinning may take place, and it is this effect which gives us a clue to how the skull was made.

On October 27, 1970, Frank Dorland and I took the skull out of the vault for some tests. The destination was Santa Clara, California, and the crystal laboratories of the Hewlett-Packard Company.

Hewlett-Packard is the world's largest manufacturer of electronic test equipment, computers and other devices. Their division in Santa Clara manufactures tiny quartz oscillators for use in time and frequency standards. Most of the quartz Hewlett-Packard uses is mined from Brazil and arrives as fist-sized rocks of various colors. The crystals are inspected, their axes determined, and then they are sliced to size. Hewlett-Packard manufactures more crystal oscillators of this type than any company in the world.

On this first visit, we arrived late in the morning and Tom Nawalinski, the division's advertising manager, introduced us to Jim Pruett, head of Hewlett-Packard's crystal labs. The labs, of course, were exactly the right place for testing quartz crystal; that is one of its day-to-day requirements. Dorland removed the skull from its case and immediately the entire department crowded around to hear his tale of the skull's mysterious past. Two engineers, Larry Mather and Buck Austin, along with two assistants, Jim Longnecker and Mike Knock, then took the skull into a laboratory designed to analyze crystals and determine their various axes prior to cutting, lapping and polishing.

Quartz is also of interest in its optical behavior, since it displays rotary polarization. When a beam of polarized light is directed through a right-handed crystal, for example, the direction of the vertical axis is to the right. A left-handed crystal rotates it toward the left.

In passing polarized light through the skull its various axes may be identified. At first, the Hewlett-Packard engineers thought the skull was a composite of three crystals, exhibiting "blackouts" or darkening of the internal regions at several rotational points. The Z axis seemed to run from the top half of the skull and extend through the lower right half of the upper part of the mouth. Considerable twinning was noticed near the eye regions and the jawbone portion showed twinning as far as the Z axis was concerned along most of its surfaces. However, the twinning was only scarcely evident during this experiment, displaying itself as a dim, rainbowlike stratum. These twinned regions seemed to be concentrated around the eyes, nose, jaw and portions of the lower skull. The upper rear portion of the skull appeared to be relatively free from such twinning.

The arrival of anything as tantalizing as the skull at Hewlett-Packard was unexpected. Many of them were vaguely familiar with it because of an article in a local newspaper's Sunday supplement. Unfortunately, we had not prepared them adequately and not only were they unprepared for its examination, but the employees at Hewlett-Packard continually bombarded Dorland with questions.

Therefore, a return visit was scheduled and more elaborate experiments were planned. The plan was to completely immerse the skull in a solution of benzyl alcohol and then view it through polarized illumination. Benzyl alcohol has the same diffraction coefficient as crystal and, therefore, when crystal is submerged into this solution, it literally becomes invisible. Then, by passing polarized light through it and rotating it in a determined manner, it would be possible to locate the axis and really observe the twinning effects inherent in the skull.

On November 27, we returned to the Hewlett-Packard labs and the skull was gently lowered into the benzyl alcohol and became invisible. The overhead lights were extinguished and a beam of bright polarized light was passed through the skull and viewed through another polarized filter.

Several hours later it was determined that the skull was indeed a *single* hunk of rock crystal, and carved with total disregard for any of its axes. In fact, it seemed to have been made with respect to the three horizontal veins, which extend diagonally from the top rear of the cranium to the eye sockets, nose and mouth regions. When the face of the skull was pointing directly away from the viewer and rotated approximately 75 degrees and then

45 degrees in a counterclockwise direction, the Z axis appeared to extend perpendicular to the body. The skull was found to be from a left-handed growing crystal.

The next experiment was to determine once and forever if Dorland's speculations were correct in assuming the jawbone was detached from the skull sometime in history.

The skull was carefully rotated in the alcohol bath so the twinned regions were the brightest. Now the entire face of the skull, viewed through a polarizing filter, exhibited a brilliant rainbow of color ranging from deep violet to a bright lime green. In a single pattern, the colors swirled around the eye sockets, nasal cavity and mouth regions in thin convolutions, distorting themselves slightly when the angle of view was changed. The effect was not unlike that of a detuned color television receiver.

To find out if the jawbone was actually severed from the skull, it was then gently inserted in place. The twinning patterns from the face of the skull continued into it with no change. It was the same piece of crystal.

The intense twinning around the carved portion of the face of the skull indicated it was roughly chipped or chiseled as the first roughing out. Later it was polished, probably by a combination of silicon sand and tiny fragments of crystal, applied and worked in a poultice. Dorland estimates this process at three hundred years of constant man-hours.

It was also interesting to note at Hewlett-Packard that the entire skull became fully illuminated when a ruby laser was directed at a point directly in the middle of the nose cavity. The effect was astonishingly beautiful.

Subsequently, Hewlett-Packard reported, "If it is phony, it's a very artistic one. Quartz crystal is extremely hard material—hard in the sense that a diamond is hard, and hard to work with. The size and clarity of the 11-pound, 7-ounce Mitchell-Hedges skull made it a rarity. The workmanship is exquisite, a compound of patient hand crafting (using sand and water to smoothly abrade the rock) and technical precision requiring an estimated 300 man-years of effort.

"'One of the guys kidded that he might be able to duplicate it if you gave him a year and $100,000.' said Jim Pruett.

"'There's no way of proving its age. A lot of the occult aura—tales of mystery and evil—that have sprung up around it could easily come from its eyes. By shifting a light source or when an observer moves his view even slightly, an infinite variety of refraction patterns can be seen. They could be quite hypnotic.

"'I look on it as a very beautiful work of art irrespective of its age or authenticity. There's no denying that.' "[20]

It would be virtually impossible today—in the time when man climbs the mountains of the moon—to duplicate this achievement. The lenses, light pipes and prisms display a technical competence that the human race only achieved recently. In fact, there is no one on the globe today who would attempt to duplicate the skull. It was carved with total disregard to the natural axis of quartz crystal and virtual disregard for the fragility of the substance itself.

The fact the lower jaw was removed from the original piece can be of great importance in piecing together its history. But, at the same time, the fact evokes more questions than answers.

nine

WHAT IT ISN'T

WHAT IS THE REAL ANSWER to the skull? Is it an elaborate
hoax perpetrated by F. A. Mitchell-Hedges himself?
Or is it a genuine archaeological find from some distant
civilization of which we know nothing? Any answer
would provide us with a scenario for a B-grade motion
picture.

In the files of Frank Dorland is an affidavit from Anna
Le Guillon Mitchell-Hedges which declares that she herself uncarthed the skull from underneath a collapsed altar
in the ruins of Lubaantún in 1927. The jawbone of the
skull was found later.

What is to say now, with the evidence that Lubaantún
is much younger than anyone previously thought, that
Mitchell-Hedges simply planted it for her to find? There

is no doubt in my mind after talking with a number of
people associated with the discovery that Anna Mitchell-
Hedges found it. Or, more directly, thinks she did. Mitchell
Hedges was extremely fond of Anna and loved her as
his very own daughter. What could make a young girl
more happy than to discover an object as wonderfully
mysterious as a solid glasslike skull? And in addition to that,
discover it in a lost Mayan city deep within the jungles of
British Honduras!

And what honors would be given to *all* of her father's
efforts on behalf of science. He was a believer in Atlantis
and here, at last, could be indisputable proof of that
legendary continent.

To suggest that someone with the reputation of Mitchell-Hedges would take part in a fraud is tantamount to
heresy. His fierce independence and lofty ideals would
make this suggestion highly unpopular. And yet the
possibility must be examined.

Dr. Frederick Dockstader, one of the world's leading
authorities on pre-Columbian and precontact art now
heads the Heye Foundation of the Museum of the American Indian in New York City. On a sunny March afternoon in 1971 I arrived at the museum and while waiting
for Dr. Dockstader busied myself on the third floor photographing some of the objects that Mitchell-Hedges removed
from the Bay Islands and Lubaantún.

Dockstader had studied the skull for a brief period of
time and had also reached the conclusion that the jawbone
was removed from the same piece of crystal and not

manufactured independently. Further, there was no doubt in his mind that Anna found the skull at Lubaantún. Dockstader's best guess is that it was used by the Indians as a religious symbol although he is not certain if it was made in the New World or the Old.

"No one," he said, "will ever know the true story. No one can prove anything except it is a very remarkable object. I know of crystal objects which have been excavated under unimpeachable circumstances. But these objects were never the size of something like the skull. I don't think rock crystal occurs that large in the area.

"There were schools of craftsmanship that the Europeans conducted to reach the Indians' arts. Instead of regular objects they carved ornate designs which were not indigenous to the taste of the Indians.

"During the time from 1575 to 1650, the art of rock crystal carving flourished in Europe. And during that period a great many Old World objects were traded back and forth at that time. Any object such as the skull would have much greater value than objects made from materials native to the area. But the most intriguing thing is that the jawbone is separated. This is most unusual and not found in skulls either in Europe or the Americas. I'm inclined to believe that it was used during the Aztec period. The possibility of the skull being Mixtec in origin seems the most probable but that probability itself is quite remote."

It was Dockstader's hope that someday Anna would give

the Mitchell-Hedges skull to the Museum of the American Indian.

Authorities are far apart on the origin of the skull. George Kennedy of the Institute of Geophysics and Planetary Physics at the University of California at Los Angeles does not think the skull came from British Honduras. "I have extremely great doubts if the skull ever came from Lubaantún. Stylistically it is reminiscent of a great number of late Aztec objects which were normally carved by Mixtec artisans in the employ of the Aztecs. The style suggests that if it were authentic Pre-Columbian, it would have to date from somewhere between 1350 and 1500. To the best of my knowledge, Lubaantún was a site abandoned around the year 800. Thus, on style grounds it's hard to believe that a late Mixtec carving would be found in a Maya site abandoned 600–700 [years] earlier."[21]

If the skull were manufactured in Europe it could certainly have been taken to South America late in the eighteenth century without any records being kept on it at all. It is also possible for Mitchell-Hedges to have obtained it somewhere in Europe or the Middle East and lugged it ten thousand miles to British Honduras for Anna to find. Such a discovery would go far in establishing him as an authority. And it would make Anna unbelievably happy.

Dorland contends that much of Mitchell-Hedges' expeditions were secretly financed by none other than William Randolph Hearst. Hearst was an avid collector of *objets d'art* for his castle at San Simeon, California. What a wonderful repository that garish place would make for the crystal skull.

But if this were true, it would certainly contradict the faith that George G. Heye, the director of the Museum of the American Indian, had in Mitchell-Hedges in 1934. Eight years after the skull was discovered and the initial publicity dwindled to a trickle, he wrote to Mitchell-Hedges:

"I assure you that this exploration work which is undertaken by your own cost, and not for private profit, but for the benefit of science, will be of the greatest interest to the British Museum and ourselves, who will benefit by your work.

"We are only too pleased to support and encourage your archeological investigations in any way within our power."[22]

It would be difficult for this writer to believe that the skull was made in Europe, purchased or stolen by Mitchell-Hedges, taken thousand of miles to British Honduras, hauled through the jungles and secreted beneath a large altar stone for Anna to find.

But, nevertheless, let's consider this as a possibility. If it were made by European craftsmen the task itself would be practically impossible. The skull was carved by hand and with total disregard to the axis of the crystal. The possiblity of it simply falling apart or cracking is enormous. But even if it were made that way, in all likelihood, the jawbone would have been made separatcly and not detached after the skull had been carved. But the experiments at Hewlett-Packard cited earlier proved beyond doubt that the jaw and cranium were of the same piece of crystal and both are oriented in the same direction.

The idea of Mitchell-Hedges taking the skull by dugout from Punta Gorda with Lady Richmond Brown, Dr. Gann and the rest is not acceptable. Some forgotten person placed it there, of course, but we shall never know who.

Frank Dorland thinks that "there is the distinct possibility that the quartz skull actually was made to order sometime in the fifteenth to eighteenth centuries. Who could have ordered it? Any one of dozens of fabulously wealthy monarchs, princes and so forth who dabbled in the occult and the unknown.

"This would, of course, explain why there are two. Any skilled craftsman receiving an order from royalty would have an extra reserve item in case something happened to the first. It would be too risky to take chances on just one. Heads rolled easily in those days.

"This could explain the fact there are no mechanical grinding marks on either of the two skulls, except I did find some traces of mechanical grinding on the faces of the teeth in the Mitchell-Hedges skull. This was undoubtedly the work of a treadmill-apparatus commonly employed in the design and crafting of tiny relieved cameos. There is no doubt that all the finishing and the polishing work was meticulously and carefully executed by traditional hand labor techniques. The jawbone could have been ordered removed at final stages as an afterthought.

"While I personally believe the Mitchell-Hedges skull is of authentic antiquity of at least a thousand or so years up to perhaps the twelve thousand years calculation, I cannot prove by any means that the skull *was not* made to order sometime in the last five hundred years and finished by hand to please some potentate who was of royal dictatorship and bent toward the psychic. There were quite a few of those."

This would account for the similarity between the Mitchell-Hedges skull and the specimen in the British Museum. But if they were made in Europe, how they got to Mexico and British Honduras will remain a mystery forever.

Is it at all possible that pre-Columbians had the skill and talent to manufacture an object out of materials as hard as quartz crystal? And would it be a skull? Pre-Columbian art is usually either highly stylistic or extremely primitive. But the Aztecs produced sculptures ranging from natural to the fantastic and the Mixtecs have been credited with an extremely good eye for symmetry.

There are examples that support the idea that they possessed ability to work gem rock in detail. At the Museo Nacional there is displayed a black granite serpent and a crystal rabbit of the Nahua culture and an Aztec grasshopper of red carnelian. In the Museo Regional de

Oaxaca there is a Mixtec cup made of rock crystal from the Monte Albán Tomb No. 7.

As to how the skull was made, four possibilities surface: (1) heat, (2) impact, (3) grinding, and (4) other means of which we know nothing.

Quartz melts at a very high temperature (oxygen-acetylene heat) so it is extremely doubtful that it was cast. However, it is possible that it was fire-polished to obtain brilliant, mirror-smooth luster. Naturally it is possible to generate high temperatures with crude materials: for example, by hot air inputs to burning coke.

But we know that the skull could have been initially carved by impact because of the twinning discovered at Hewlett-Packard. Then too, Indians were extremely skillful in shaping objects by impact. But quartz is so hard, it would take an enormous amount of time to grind it efficiently, especially since South America has no deposits of carborundum and no apparent knowledge of grinding wheels.

And as to the other means? From time to time it has been suggested that the Indians used the juice of a rare plant to soften the rock used in building their temples until it could be molded to exact shapes. This would account for the way the Indians matched the joints with such precision that they could be fitted together without mortar.

It is the opinion of the American archaeologist A. Hyatt Verrill, who devoted thirty years of research to the cultures of Central and South America, that these peoples did not use cutting tools in their great constructions. Instead they used a kind of paste handed down from ancient times, to eat into the rock. Given the tools and the stone implements so far unearthed by us he concluded that no living man, Indian or otherwise, could duplicate the stone carvings. It would not be a question of skill, patience or time. It would simply be impossible. If a rock-softening paste was used, no proof of it ever existing is available to us today.

There is no evidence strong enough to the contrary to indicate that, in fact, the skull was not found by Anna at Lubaantún where it had resided for untold centuries. And it is the product of a civilization which possessed a crystallographical ability equivalent to ours today.

This conclusion is inescapable in view of the fact that the skull was hand carved with total disregard to its natural axis, found in Lubaantún, and possessed an intricate system of prisms, light-pipes, lenses and other reflective devices built into it. As a crystallographer from Hewlett-Packard said, "the damn thing simply shouldn't even be."

AN EYE TO THE ELSEWHERE?

ANNA LE GUILLON MITCHELL-HEDGES: "Sometimes I am sorry I did not inter the skull with my father as he wished. I think that may have been the best place for it. It is a thing of evil in the wrong hands.

"My father believed that the Skull brought death only to those who did not revere it, who laughed and jeered at it. He lived for thirty years after he first found and took possession of the skull. During that time he survived eight bullet wounds and three knife attacks. He did not pray to the skull, but he treated it with the same reverence that he believed the priests of the Mayan civilization had for the skull. After all, to them it was almost akin to a god.

"I believe that anyone can will another to death through

the Skull of Doom. When I sell it I want it rather to go to a museum or something like that where it can do no harm to anyone. I am not afraid of the skull, for I revere it as my late father did, but I am afraid of the harm the skull can do if it gets into the wrong hands."[23]

Frank Dorland: "The first time I kept the skull in my home overnight, having worked too late to take it back to the bank vault, my wife and I were awakened by unusual noises in the house. It sounded as if a large jungle cat was prowling through the house, accompanied by the sound of chimes and bells. When we got up the next morning, our possessions were strewn all about the house. Yet, all the doors and windows were still closed and locked from the inside."

From a South African newspaper: "'The Skull of Doom' . . . notorious for the bad luck it brings to those who view it, left another victim in its wake when it passed through East London in the Stirling Castle today. . . .

"Within a few hours of photographing the skull, Mr. Jack Ramsden, a newspaper cameraman, had the shock of his life when he started to make a print from the negative. As he switched on the apparatus there was a shattering explosion and the already darkened room was plunged into complete darkness. 'I ran from the room and nothing would take me back. . . . In my twenty years as a photographer I have never known this to happen to an enlarger. They have flickered and gone out but I have never even heard of one exploding like this.'

"Mr. Mitchell-Hedges maintains that the skull is the embodiment of all evil. It was used by the high priest of the Maya civilization before 1600 B.C. Legend says he took the skull into the depths of the temple and concentrated on it, willing death. Death always comes to someone connected with it."

Letter to F. A. Mitchell-Hedges, October 25, 1949:

"Dear Mr. Mitchell-Hedges,

I am writing to let you know that your souvenir, 'The Skull of Doom' will be much sought after by the Zulu Sangunas and will probably be stolen very soon.

"You will have read that members of the Zulu Royal House were struck by lightning. This will be associated with the return of 'Zulu'* by the so-called medicine man. Your harmless souvenir will be smelt out as a valuable organizing factor in nature insurrection—in fact, it is from a native point of view more powerful than 'Stalin.'

"I am not interested one way or another in superstition, but can definitely say that I feel you must be careful, otherwise your trinkets can cause a great deal of trouble in Africa."

Yours Sincerely,
Clifford M. Hulley
Home Farm, Ixopo

* The skull in this case.

Alameda County Weekender: "Anton Szandor LaVey thinks the most important function of the Mitchell-Hedges skull was to serve as a sort of memory bank, somewhat on the order of those in our most sophisticated computers. How it could serve in that fashion, while admittedly obscure to nonmagicians, is not so preposterous as it sounds. The skull is filled with planes and striations in the crystal, some of which have the effect of a lens. In looking into the skull for any length of time an effect is received that is far greater and vastly more complex than that received from a crystal ball. Since even a crystal ball will have a psychic effect on whoever looks into it, if he looks long enough—and so would a glass of water—and since no force can be exerted without an equal and opposite one, it is at least theoretically possible that the crystal skull, over centuries of use, has been affected by the generations of priests who must have gazed into it for purposes of divination. Though LaVey, who has examined the skull extensively on several occasions, feels that psychometry—the business of learning the history of an object by sensing vibrations from it—generally reveals nothing more than what is already in the mind of the psychometrist, he is of the definite opinion that the crystal skull is easily the most valuable find yet known in that section of the archeological field dealing with matters of magic.

"In this respect, he finds it as 'powerful corroborating evidence' of what he terms 'The Law of the Trapezoid' . . . which can be briefly described as a theory that certain geometrical patterns—in particular the trapezoidal one presented by a truncated pyramid—have an immensely powerful, adverse effect on the human mind, leading to at least mental and emotional imbalance."[24]

Fate Magazine: "After Mitchell-Hedges said that his tests had shown the temperature of the skull never changes, other authorities found that whatever temperature the skull was subjected to, it maintained a steady temperature of about 70° Fahrenheit. When it was placed in a refrigerator at a temperature of 28° below zero it came out showing a reading of 70°."[25]

Anna Le Guillon Mitchell-Hedges: "I wonder why people always have to theorize as how or from where we got the Rock Crystal Skull. As I told Frank Dorland we found it in Lubaantún in Central America, and were told by the few remaining Maya, that it was Mayan . . . that it had taken five generations to rub down with sand, and was used by the high priest to will death. . . . "I WILL NOT HAVE THE SKULL USED AS A CRYSTAL BALL."[26]

Now that the skull has been returned to Anna Mitchell-Hedges such spiritualistic goings-on will probably cease. But in the years prior to her repossession of the skull, a crowd of psychics, both sincere and otherwise, have attempted to "read" the skull's history from the work itself. Strangely, there is little variation in what they have concluded although both the readings and the psychics themselves were screened from one another. What Dorland has distilled from all this is that the symbolism of the skull, its age, its beauty and rarity, show that ancient man was not only deeply religious but also believed that there was one and only one super God who rules the universe.

"The supranatural properties of the skull are puzzling, of course," says Dorland, "but they are very much in existence and are demonstrable to any sensitive person. The skull exhibits and transmits to the human brain all the five senses: taste, touch, smell, sight and hearing. The skull changes visibly in color and transparency, it exhibits its own unmistakable odor when it cares to, it plants thoughts in viewers' minds, it makes people thirsty, it impresses audible sounds on the ears of viewers, to those in meditation before the skull, they feel all this and they also feel physical pressures on their faces and bodies. When a sensitive person places his hands near the skull, distinct feelings of vibrations and energy are felt and the senses of both heat and cold depending on where the hands are held."

I asked Dorland to elaborate on his claim that the skull transmits physical sensations to human beings.

"As far as sight is concerned, the skull seems to be constantly in a state of flux, exhibiting changes of mood, clarity and color. The front part of the skull has been observed to turn cloudy like soft cotton candy. The very center of the skull sometimes turns so absolutely clear it seems to disappear into a vast void. The skull itself in total has changed in color from clear crystal to shades of green, violet, purple, amber, red, blue, etc. The visual study of the skull has strong tendencies to exert hypnotic effects on the majority of viewers. On at least one occasion, the skull developed a radiating aura that was in existence and very evident for at least a time of six minutes, allowing not lengthy, but quite accurate studies of its appearance.

"Numerous sounds have been heard by many observers; the most usual sounds so far, have been rhythmic tinkling of high-pitched chimes or bells and a polyphonia-like chorus of what sounds to be many soft human voices. There have been unexplained thumps, cracking and snapping noises and various other sounds which may or may not have had any relation at all to the presence of the skull.

"Touch or physical feel or sensation, not necessarily in the fingertips as very very few individuals have ever been allowed to go so far as the actual fingertip exploration of the skull. Most sensations have been reported as the pulling of the eyes or a sensation in the back of the eye sockets, a tightness through the chest area, a tightening of the arm and leg muscles or tendons. Observations have shown that these feelings have frequently been accompanied by an accelerated pulse and rise in blood pressure usually noticeable in pulsing at both sides of the throat. On occasions, there has been a most distinctive and elusive perfume or odor, most difficult to compare with any of the more commonly known odors. It is perhaps best described as a fleeting odor, with a velvety smooth heavy earth-type muskiness with a high accent note that is both bitter and acid. Taste, the last of the five senses, has not been in particular evidence so far.

"Probably the most important thing the skull did while it was in my care was to show me that most living things and many material things are surrounded by a halo or aura or whatever you want to call it.

"Before I had the skull in my possession and actually saw for myself, time after time, the aura that the skull presented, I thought that anyone seeing auras needed to have their eyes checked or their head examined.

"Now, my eyes are examined regularly as a necessary part of my profession. I have five pairs of glasses for various corrections, my camera eyepieces have corrective lenses, my microscopes are corrected and checked. I am positive that my eyes are functioning properly.

"The skull has taught me how and where to see the aura. I can swear that it's a true fact that people really are surrounded by some substance that is visible and can really be seen if you just look for it in the right manner.

"This has taught me that when early religious artists painted halos and surrounded the heads of the saints and other religious figures with bands of radiance and light, they were not a figment of their imagination. I am sure that many of these artists actually depicted what they saw. Of course, later on the painters simply copied earlier trends and this developed into the traditional ringed halo which probably never existed.

"When I first saw the aura around the skull, it had become quite radiant and surrounded the skull about 18 inches away in all directions. It was impossible to believe. I picked up a magazine and read some of the print to focus my eyes and looked back at the skull. Sure enough, there was no aura. But then as I kept looking, the aura grew again and increased in intensity. This was the secret. My eyes could not be in focus on sharp edges and outlines to see the aura. I had to focus on *soft* indistinct things. My eyes had to focus into space where there was supposedly nothing but invisible air.

"I think that has something to do with seeing auras. We are taught as children to focus on the hard edge of things, to see and focus our eyes on outlines of letters in order to read words. And most children's books are illustrated with hard-edge drawings. We need to reassemble our mental thinking and focus on things that are not hard-edge items when we wish to see, substantially, other worlds and other things."

Naturally it is as easy to read images in crystal as it is to see characters in clouds. Patterns diffuse and dissolve with the slightest change in viewing angle or illumination. And many claim that the skull becomes cloudy or changes color when it is used as a speculum for crystallomancy. There is no question that in most cases these are probably an illusion, but such illusions are commonplace to the Dorlands.

Dorland told of one time, on a cool July evening, that

six people were scheduled to arrive and examine the skull. Among the six was a psychiatrist, a minister, and a "sensitive."

Dorland had carefully cleaned the skull earlier that afternoon, a procedure they followed each time the skull was shown. They felt cleaning was necessary to ensure the skull would be free of any foreign manner. And so the sparkling skull was placed on its stand which contained a concealed microscope illuminator inside its hollow interior.

Duplicating the procedure they believed was used centuries ago, the lamp was pointed up through the base of the skull. Later that evening, with the guests sitting silently around the skull, it happened. The room lights had long been turned off and the skull glowed in the gentle radiance from the tiny lamp—a visual magnet. As they watched, the forehead of the skull gradually turned cloudy, then milky white. Frank changed his position to shift his view. The forehead looked as though it had been stuffed with cotton. He glanced at his wife, Mabel, and she nodded.

A small darkish spot then appeared on the side of the skull near its temple. The spot slowly increased in size and intensity. "I studied the faces of our six guests and was easily able to determine that they too were seeing activity within the skull," says Dorland. "It was an obvious fact that each one of the eight people in the room were witnessing a spontaneous optical phenomenon. I gazed again at the skull and silently watched as the dark area increased in size until it appeared that the major portion of the center mass of the skull had simply dissolved and vanished.

"The outlines of the skull were as evident as ever but the mid section of the solid crystal rock had vanished into a void of nothingness. There just wasn't anything there, not a thing. The skull was acting like a window into unknown space, a porthole looking into a world elsewhere.

"I remembered reading in some old treatises on oracles and crystal gazing that when the veils lift, the prophecies of truth then appear. Were we seeing the lifting of the veils? I believe that we were.

"Our guests lingered on, the skull had returned to its normal appearance. We had switched on the room lights and we carefully inspected the skull, the stand and the light beneath it. All was in perfect order. There was nothing amiss."

Later, over cups of hot coffee, a lively discussion arose about the evening's episode. Each person there had witnessed the same thing with minor personal variations. There was no doubt but that each one saw, in his own way, a drastic visible change in the appearance of the crystal skull.

"Some months later, Mabel and I obtained the loan of an authentic antique rock crystal ball from the history division of the Oakland Public Museum. We were overjoyed as the crystal ball had similar flaws and veils to those in the skull. This would enable us to make a good comparison study of the two.

"We kept the rock crystal ball with the skull for two

years of experiments. We were fascinated to discover that
the museum's specimen eventually reproduced in a lesser
degree, some of the identical phenomena so outstanding
in the Mitchell-Hedges skull. We did not hear any sounds,
music or tinkling bells from the ball, but we did see the
lifting of the veils, the visions, and smelled the sweet-sour
odor emanating from it."

So there, laid to the barest bone, are the inexplicable
phenomena attributed to the crystal skull by Frank Dorland and others. Although I have never been able to
witness any of these phenomena, the possiblity that these
"tricks" may be the result of intense concentration and
meditation cannot be ruled out. The hypnotic effects
the skull transmits—particularly when it is illuminated—
could easily induce trance states to easily susceptible or
sensitive persons. But the claims that the crystal skull has
caused or can cause death should most likely be filed
right next to the curses of old King Tut.

At 8 A.M. on June 12, 1959, F. A. Mitchell-Hedges
died of a cerebral embolism, and he was cremated and his
ashes scattered at sea. Except for a brief period of time
in 1928–1929 when the skull was used as collateral for
a loan, it never left his possession. When Mitchell-Hedges
traveled the skull went with him. At home in Farley
Castle, thirty-six miles west of London, it was kept at
bedside.

Anna, now in her late sixties, lives with her two Pekin-
ese at the motel she owns in Ontario, Canada. She has
long since sold Farley Castle and placed many of her

valuables in storage. Even to this day she claims that she alone knows the location of the fortune of Henry Morgan, Britain's most terrible buccaneer. In November 1970, she retrieved the skull from Dorland and returned with it to Canada. Early in 1972, she lent it to the Museum of the American Indian (Heye Foundation) in New York where it may or may not become a permanent display.

On matters of psychic phenomena I remain an agnostic. There can be little doubt in my mind that the skull during its hazy history had been used as an oracle and in other forms of divination. If the images are coincidental then that is that. If the pictures of the observatory and truncated pyramid are the result of some sort of crystalline stabilization caused by magical practices then the scientific ramifications would be spectacular if not revolutionary. Many many hours of tests and examination should be given this unique object under highly controlled conditions. Findings could result in a tremendous advancement of human knowledge.

Whether it be ESP, psychic phenomena or whatever, within the last four hundred years we have witnessed several remarkable successes in organizing "unknowables" into scientific patterns. Galileo's conception of the solar system, Mendeleev's ordering of the basic elements into the periodic table, Faraday's structuring of the properties of electricity, Einstein's all-embracing theories of motion, time and mass have this in common: By finding a unifying theory, each enabled mankind not only to know why things behaved the way they did, but to benefit him in practical, bread-and-butter improvements in his way of life.

So we could pose the question: Could the crystal skull represent another breakthrough in man's knowledge of his universe? Can another Newton formulate a comprehensive theory to bring order out of the chaos of mystical and paraspiritual beliefs which have had their own population explosion in our era?

Yet we must remind ourselves that we are not speaking here of a scientific advance of quite the same level as what we have just chronicled. In this, the scientifically knowable was that theory or phenomenon that could be held in the "net" of logical and repeatable demonstrations. But the darkened room we are now trying to enter is not the same sort of unexplored area: the object of our search is really the mind itself.

In the vast view of the universe, nothing moves—not a particle—without displacing every other particle to some extent. The blink of an eye jars the cosmos.

And the effects of distant disturbances surround us every day of our lives. Retreat into a dark closet, flick on a transistor radio, and the subtle bumps made into thin air a hundred miles distant reverberate into a cacophony of sound—or, more pointedly, not a cacophony, a symphony. Can these delicate vibrations, capable of transmitting the faintest whisper, be any more believable (just because we give them electromagnetic voices) than the vibrations that supposedly emanate from a restless mind?

From time to time, individuals who are blessed with such perceptiveness crash into the headlines. A little girl is kidnaped; the police are baffled. In desperation a seer is called in to attempt to locate the child. The reputation of Madame von Strahl was considerably enhanced when she assisted a sheriff in northern California in such an endeavor. The noted psychic Peter Hurkos had been called in to help solve the brutal slaying of actress Sharon Tate and her companions.

If there is a breakthrough in explaining the way the mind interacts with the cosmos, to what extent will the results be more than circular? Philosophers have characterized the human intellect as being distinctive in its ability to reflect upon itself. It is a noble thought, but the results of that reflection have also resembled a dog chasing his tail.

The crudest forms of psychic adventures, including astrology, have been seized upon by a whole generation of "seekers" who have lost confidence in the pat answers of their elders. The widespread use of mind-expanding drugs is a phenomenon of our times whose proportions are not matched anywhere in recorded history. In the "straight" world too, a revolutionary course has been charted for the human psychic by the perfection of the techniques of mass communication, of data processing, and of the psychical alteration of the nervous system. We have a twentieth-century form of numerology in our opinion polls, stock market charts and computerized merchandising. The prophets are clean-shaven young men in white short-sleeved shirts; their divining rods are pocket calculators.

The blind are enabled to "see," the armless are enabled to "touch," by direct manipulation of the sensory apparatus of the brain. When brain transplants become feasible (if they do), the definition of what a person *is* will also require some transplanting.

Out of a disenfranchisement of the young from our scientific republic has sprung a host of paradoxes. These ultimate realists, in the afterglow of the age of reason and of scientific sanctification, have espoused all the elements of nonreason, of what Arthur Koestler calls a "congenitally disordered mental condition" caused by the conflict of two parts of the mind that have evolved separately but not equally.

Putting it in its baldest form, Koestler urges the physiological theory that there is a schizophrenic split between reason and emotion caused by the fact that the emotions are evolutionary hand-me-downs from lower mammals and reptiles, while the neocortex, the "thinking cap" of the brain, is a fast-breaking development which has far outstripped its horse-and-buggy counterparts. The immediate advantage of this theory is that it readily explains the aberrations some people see, hear, feel or smell around the crystal skull.

Organized religion—an excellent barometer of the changing behavioral climate—knows well that objects need to be venerated and given magical properties. And the straight-faced fairy tales of Graham Greene—of mad priests consecrating the entire contents of a bakery into the Body and Blood of the Savior—may still be a stale joke on a magic-prone generation.

If an Einstein could have appeared on the scene in the last two decades to find order in this religious-metaphysical-mystic mix, it might have been Aldous Huxley. At the world's great universities, he lectured on the "immortality of the soul" in terms of modern psychology and ESP. In private and in his writings, he brought to bear on the subject a compendium of knowledge about psychic experiments and theories unequaled at any other single source. His conclusion was that it was too late to ask whether psychic phenomena exist; but not too early to ask how and why.

Scientific inquiry has now become a hotbed for a new development of the nonscientific uses of the mind. It is no longer a contradiction in terms to speak of a non-scientific use of the mind. The psychic leap and the act of faith are no longer considered aberrations, but natural propensities of the intellect.

There is a feeling in the air that the age of reason is long dead, that a new era of the exploration of human consciousness is unfolding all around us. The obvious manifestations of the moment—mind-expanding drugs, revolution as a social luxury, the information cult—are not nearly so convincing in themselves as the simple fact that conventional science is uncovering wherever it turns—at the limts of its explorations of nuclear physics, astronomy, or psychology—blank walls of resistance that the tools of the past cannot penetrate.

The tendency to debunk anything foreign to us—in thought or geography—is so strong that conscientious newspapers must constantly bend over backward in an attempt to be objective. At the other extreme, the devotees of an occult theory usually avoid any pretense of coming to terms with conventional science. The believers in the flat-earth theory allowed that photographs of the earth from space were a challenge to their argument. But their society did not disband. In fact, we can probably expect, rather than a readjustment of their basic tenets, a proposed revision of their theory of photography.

Our hemispheres are teeming with mysteries. But we pass through a world in which mysteries and riddles of every size and shape must be ignored as we go about the little necessities of daily living. The pyramids, the weird lines stretching for miles on the plateau above the Nazca Valley, the strange, prophetic maps of the Turkish Admiral Piri Risi, the great empires of the Mayas are items which only occasionally invite our curiosity. And we accept them most of our lives without so much as an acknowledgment to their significance—like rodents making nests in the ruins of a cathedral.

And we are left with a beautiful quartz crystal eye to the elsewhere, carved in the form of a human skull and very possibly a time bomb in the history of science.

NOTES

1. *Man,* published by the Royal Anthropological Institute of Great Britain and Ireland, July 1936.

2. *Ibid.*

3. *Ibid.*

4. *Ibid.*

5. *Ibid.*

6. *Ibid.*

7. *Ibid.*

8. *Ibid.*

9. Letter to author from Mr. Digby, November 22, 1970.

10. *New York American,* March 10, 1935.

11. F. A. Mitchell-Hedges, *Danger My Ally* (Boston: Little, Brown and Company, 1955).

12. *Ibid.*

13. *Ibid.*

14. Mitchell-Hedges, *op. cit.*

15. *New York American,* August 31, 1930.

16. *New York American,* February 10, 1935.

17. *Ibid.*

18. Sibley S. Morrill, "The Skull Motif and Mayan Discovery of Zero," *Indian Historian,* June 1968.

19. Sylvanus G. Morley, *The Ancient Maya* (Stanford, Calif.: Stanford University Press, 1968).

20. *Measure,* Hewlett-Packard Company, February 1971.

21. Letter to Frank Dorland from George Kennedy, February 1971.

22. Letter from George Heye to Mitchell-Hedges, January 25, 1934.

23. *Fate Magazine,* March 1962.

24. *Alameda County Weekender,* Morning News and Times Star, October 3, 1966.

25. *Fate Magazine, op. cit.*

26. Letter to author from Anna Mitchell-Hedges, January 30, 1970.